CROTON POINT
PARK

WESTCHESTER'S
JEWEL ON THE HUDSON

SCOTT CRAVEN & CAROLINE RANALD CURVAN

THE
History
PRESS

Published by The History Press
Charleston, SC
www.historypress.com

First published 2022

Manufactured in the United States

ISBN 9781467152389

Library of Congress Control Number: 2022936206

CONTENTS

LAND ACKNOWLEDGEMENT

We would like to acknowledge that we are learning, writing about and gathering on the ancestral homeland of the Munsee-speaking Kitchawanc people, who are the Indigenous peoples of Croton Point. Despite tremendous hardship in being forced from here, today many from their community reside in Wisconsin, Oklahoma and Ontario. We invite you to join us in paying respect to the Indigenous peoples still connected to this land as we commit to building a more inclusive and equitable space for all.

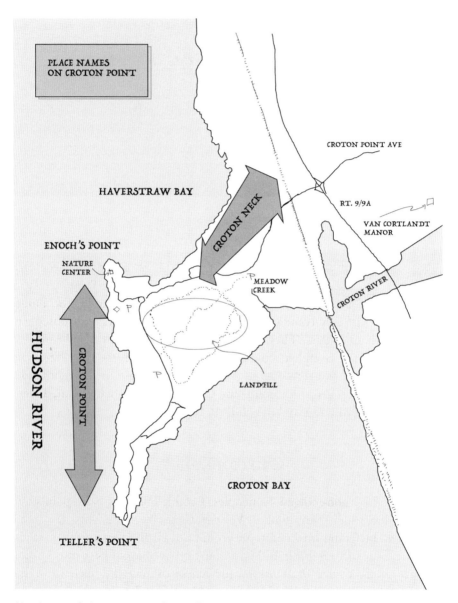

PLACE NAMES
ON CROTON POINT

HAVERSTRAW BAY

CROTON POINT AVE

CROTON NECK

RT. 9/9A

VAN CORTLANDT
MANOR

ENOCH'S POINT

NATURE
CENTER

MEADOW
CREEK

CROTON RIVER

HUDSON RIVER

CROTON POINT

LANDFILL

CROTON BAY

TELLER'S POINT

Sketch map of place names on Croton Point. *Map by Harrison Isaac.*

PREFACE

M ost of the place names we use in this book are not those used by the Indigenous people who were displaced from this land. While some are based on the indigenous names, the names used today primarily come to us from European explorers and subsequent Euro-American settlers. They recorded what they thought they heard in a language that was completely unfamiliar to them, so misunderstandings and mistakes abound. For purposes of this book, we will use the current names noted on the map here—Croton Point, Croton Neck, Enoch's Point, Teller's Point, the Croton River and the Hudson River.

CROTON POINT

As mapped by non-indigenous peoples, Croton Point, its bays, points and beaches have had many names. We don't exactly know when the name Croton Point came into common use, although the first mention seems to have been on an 1839 U.S. Coastal Survey map. The name Croton is believed to derive from *Kenoten* (or *Knoten* or *Noten*), a sachem of the Kitchawanc meaning "Wild Wind" or "The Wind."

Today, when people speak about "Croton Point," they are usually referring to the County Park or at least that part of the ancient peninsula that is west of the modern railroad tracks. Geologically however, this landform extends as far east as Riverside Avenue and Van Cortlandt Manor. Most of that land was excavated and removed in the nineteenth and twentieth centuries for fill and to allow corridors for roads and railroads.

The first land transaction document we have, from 1682 between Cornelius van Bursum and twenty "Indian proprietors,"[1] used indigenous names for several locations on and near today's Croton Point:

- NAVISH specifically describes the sandy plateau you see on your right as you enter the park, part of today's Croton Neck.

- SENASQUA (possibly derived from *wanasqua*, meaning "point") and Croton Neck, the salt marsh (now obscured by the capped landfill) and maybe even Enoch's Point.

- TANRACKEN describes the creek that cut through the neck, today known as Meadow Creek. Like the salt marsh, much of this creek has been buried by the landfill. However, at high tide, you can kayak into the mouth of what's left of this creek from the Croton River side and explore several hundred feet into the swamp.

BEACH AREAS

Authors' note: Dates in parentheses indicates first documented use of name.

Today's park beach area (facing Haverstraw Bay) has variously been called Wash Banks (1839), Teller's Cove (1854) and Mother's Lap (1898). Just to make things confusing, the coastline along the Hudson and between the two points has also been called Mother's Lap (1839). Most recently, in 1931, it was dubbed Squaw Cove.

MORE HISTORY OF NAMES

Enoch's Point was also called Senasqua (1682), Enock's [*sic*] Point (1775), Teller's Point North (1854), Northwest Point (1898) and Enoch's Neck (1914). However, we have no idea who Enoch was or why this point was named after him.

Teller's Point was named after the Teller family, who were probably the first Europeans to live there. It was also known as Sarah's Point and, on an 1854 map, Teller's Point South.

OTHER LOCAL NAMES

The Hudson River was named after Henry Hudson, the first European to document sailing up the river in 1609. It was also regularly called the North River up through the Revolutionary War era. However, it's important to note that there were many indigenous names for this river. Flowing for about 315 miles from Lake Tear of the Clouds in the Adirondacks down to the Atlantic Ocean, it passes through the homelands of several Indian nations, and each had a name for it. While we will use the current name, know that the Indigenous people on and around Croton Point would have called it Mahicannittuk (Mohicans) or Muhheakantuck (Lenapes). Both names are often translated to mean "river that flows both ways," a nod to the tidal nature of the river.

Kitchawanc is what the Croton River was originally called. It is also the name of the Indigenous people who lived on Croton Point.

Dr. Jonathan Lothrop, curator of archaeology, New York State Museum, not only spent a great deal of time on the phone clarifying what is currently known of early peoples in New York State, but he also gave us access to artifacts in storage at the NYSM.

Sandra Michael told us the story of her grandparents Thomas and Minnie Nabors, who had actually lived and worked on Croton Point, and she kindly took the time to unearth and get a high-quality scan of her photograph of them. Thanks also to her nephew Dwayne Mann for putting us in touch.

Thomas P. Musante helped us with image formatting.

Carl Oeschner, local history legend and storyteller extraordinaire, graciously opened his voluminous files on Croton Point to us.

Patrick Persons spent time in the Westchester County Archives pulling early deeds of land transfers on Croton Point for us.

Arnold Pickman, of Cragsmoor Consultants, generously gave us access to the full Cultural Resources Survey Report on Croton Point from 2004.

Charlie Roberto, for introducing thousands of people to Croton Point's bald eagles.

Ken Sargeant, co-director of the Harlem Cultural Archives, shared his extensive knowledge of Theodore Cornu, Henry Gourdine and the story of Robert William Justice, giving us unique insights into the Black experience on Croton Point. (Find him on YouTube at River Liver Productions.)

Joyce Sharrock-Cole, village historian of Ossining, gave us details, insight and support.

Anne Swain, executive director of the Saw Mill River Audubon Society, graciously shared her knowledge about the wildlife on Croton Point.

Sarah Underhill, a direct descendant of the Underhills of Croton Point, shared photos and documents that helped us flesh out the story of her family.

Robert van der Linden, PhD, curator of air transportation and special purpose aircraft at the Smithsonian National Air and Space Museum, identified the Curtiss aircraft in our photo, putting to rest the story that the Wright brothers had landed on Croton Point.

Thanks to Jim Wall for identifying Judge Frank Decker's Stutz Bearcat.

Carol Weed, MA (RPA), thoughtfully contributed her professional expertise regarding archaeological matters and the way the early people on and around Croton Point lived.

Dana White and Dorian Burden kindly read through early chapters, giving us needed feedback.

Gene Panczenko's artistic photos of the Underhill wine cellars were a last-minute and fortuitous gift from the universe.

A special thanks goes to Harrison Isaac, who took our hand-drawn scribbles and confusing notes and created maps of clarity and insight.

Finally, we'd like to thank our families for putting up with our endless stories of bricks and grapes, rocks and oyster shells. John Curvan went above and beyond, hiking and kayaking every inch of the point in all weathers.

Thanks to Mary Craven, Scott's long-suffering wife and the Queen of Scott's river, who handled this latest Hudson Valley project with grace and aplomb.

Again, thanks to the community of experts who did all they could to help us get the facts right. Any errors or inaccuracies are ours alone.

SC and CC

INTRODUCTION

Outside lies utterly ordinary space open to any casual explorer willing to find the extraordinary. Outside lies unprogrammed awareness that at times becomes serendipity. Outside lies magic.
—John Stilgoe

The real voyage of discovery consists, not in seeking new landscapes, but in having new eyes.
—Marcel Proust

A fifty-five-minute train ride from New York City puts you at the threshold of Croton Point Park. Here, you will find the entire history of the Hudson Valley hidden in plain sight in this accessible and well-supported spot.

The relationship between the urban and the suburban is etched here, as the modern point has been shaped by the demands of New York City—from the sand excavated to permit transportation corridors to the bricks mined and fired here to build the city and to the wine and fruit exported.

Ultimately becoming a dumping ground for Westchester County, Croton Point has borne the brunt of two centuries of defacement and serves as a warning about the environmental implications of our way of life. But the story of Croton Point is ultimately one of redemption and inspiration. Despite the ruin it has suffered, its life as a park today is a model of inclusivity and environmental stewardship.

We wrote this book to reveal this treasure to you by sharing its stories and personally connecting you to the history of the Hudson Valley in a compact, easily digestible way. Ultimately, we hope to give you some background that will activate your own innate curiosity and encourage you to look, wonder and learn.

Here are just some of the things you can see on Croton Point:

- Boulders that were transported here by a sheet of ice during the glacial era of the Hudson Valley.

- A ten-thousand-year-old artifact that was fashioned by an Archaic person who lived here millennia before Europeans arrived.

- Shell mounds that give us more tangible evidence of the people and cultures that preceded European colonization.

- The very spot where the American Revolution turned with the interruption of Benedict Arnold's plot to sell the plans of West Point to British major John André.

- The remains of one of the first commercial vineyards in the Northeast.

- Bricks left over from one of the many brickyards that built New York City.

- 10.4 million cubic yards of municipal waste that continues to be mitigated and repurposed thanks to the success of the modern environmental movement.

As the writer and environmentalist Wendell Berry said, "Nobody can discover the world for somebody else. Only when we discover it for ourselves does it become common ground and a common bond and we cease to be alone." With the knowledge you glean from this book, we hope that you will see Croton Point and the entire Hudson Valley in a new light and become part of an ever-growing community that enjoys this beautiful piece of land.

Croton Point belongs to all of us, and it's up to all of us to maintain and preserve it for future generations.

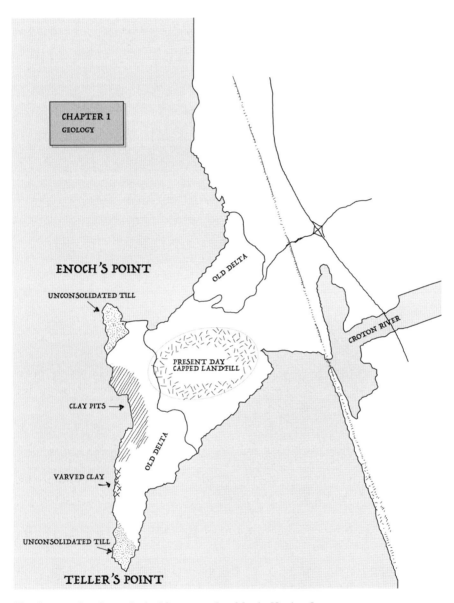

CHAPTER 1
GEOLOGY

ENOCH'S POINT

UNCONSOLIDATED TILL

OLD DELTA

CROTON RIVER

PRESENT DAY
CAPPED LANDFILL

CLAY PITS

OLD DELTA

VARVED CLAY

UNCONSOLIDATED TILL

TELLER'S POINT

Sketch map of major geological features today. *Map by Harrison Isaac.*

Chapter 1

GEOLOGY

Born of fire, carved by ice, finessed with wind, water and snow.
—Anne Shepherd, The Living Mountain

Croton Point, at its most basic level, is a peninsula, surrounded on three sides by water and attached to a larger landmass. Formed of materials that were born billions of years ago, on a river whose origins go back to a time when the Hudson River Valley was situated on the equator, Croton Point was, in geological terms, shaped yesterday by the last series of glaciers to travel down this valley.

If an interested visitor to the valley were to embark on a quest for glacial evidence along the Hudson River, a lot of the evidence would be too big to comprehend. Examples of this include the Verrazzano Narrows, the jagged course of the river through the Highlands, and the terminal moraine that is Long Island. And a lot of the evidence would also be too small to pay attention to: chatter-marks on Bear Mountain rock faces, glacial striations on rocks in New York City's Central Park, the different types of sand on the shore of the Hudson River and more.

On Croton Point, the work of the glaciers is concentrated and easily seen. First, it's necessary to understand that Croton Point comprises two separate and distinct glacial landforms. Projecting out from the mainland, perpendicular to the river, is "Croton Neck." Crossing that "T" at the end of the neck is "Croton Point." Both were created at different times during the last glacial episode by two distinctly different mechanisms.

GEOLOGICAL TERMS

delta: A nearly flat tract of land at or near the mouth of a river, resulting from the accumulation of sediment (Croton Neck). A *hanging delta* is an exposed delta left behind when the water level lowers (Croton Neck Plateau).

drumlin: A low, smoothly rounded, elongated hill, mound or ridge of compact glacial till (Teller's to Enoch's Points).

terminal moraine: Pile of rubble left at the farthest reach of a glacier (Long Island).

till: Unconsolidated mixture of clay, sand, pebbles, boulders and rock debris deposited by and underneath a glacier (Croton Point).

tombolo: A sand or gravel barrier that connects an island with the mainland. (Croton Neck, before the landfill, was all that connected Croton Point to the mainland.)

varve: A sedimentary layer deposited in still water within one year's time, characterized in glacial lakes by alternating light and dark bands (Croton Point's varved clay beds).

Confusing the issue is the one-hundred-foot-tall mountain that sits right in the middle of it all. Made by humans, not glaciers, it is the now-capped landfill that once absorbed much of the garbage of Westchester County from 1924 to 1985. Also, the fact that at least half of the peninsula has been quarried away vastly affects our perception of this landform.

CROTON NECK: THE OLD DELTA

From the very moment you even approach the park, a vast geological story will be laid out in front of you, if you know what you're seeing.

The first thing you will see is a seventy-foot-high plateau, with tall trees on top—called Navish by the Indigenous peoples and Croton Neck today.

Exposed delta cross section. Note the level of the old glacial lake. *Croton Historical Society.*

This plateau was once part of the delta of a great, ancient lake and is our introduction to how much Croton Point and the Hudson River have changed over the last twenty-five thousand years.

When the last ice sheet began retreating, it left behind a huge dam (or, more accurately, a terminal moraine) at the foot of the Hudson River Valley, stretching across today's Verrazzano Narrows from Staten Island to Brooklyn. All the glacier's meltwater was captured, creating long, massive lakes that stretched as far north as present-day Albany.

At the same time, various tributaries, such as the ancient Croton River, were flowing like Yoohoo from a fire hose as they entered the lakes. Filled with sand and super-fine rock flour from the grinding bottom of the ice sheets, these torrents deposited sediment that created deltas when they entered the lake. And that flat-topped sandy plateau at the entrance to Croton Point Park is what remains of the ancient delta created by the Croton River.

Today, it stands far above the river, vividly illustrating that the water level was once fifty to seventy feet higher than it is today. Combine this with the fact that the land has been rising slowly since the glacier left, a phenomenon called isostatic rebound, and we'll begin to understand how different this spot would have looked at the end of the last ice age.

WHERE DID THE LAKES GO? AND WHY IS THE WATER LEVEL SO MUCH LOWER TODAY?

About fourteen thousand years ago, as the glaciers were slinking back to their northern lairs, above what is now New York State, they unleashed Glacial Lake Iroquois. Monstrous in size and covering two of our modern Great Lakes, this giant lake poured down the future Hudson River Valley on a biblical scale. Robert and Johanna Titus, in their book *The Hudson Valley in the Ice Age*, describe an "88-day flood of over 160 cubic miles of water raging at a speed of 120 million gallons of water per second."[2] (To put this into perspective, today the river flows downstream at approximately 135,000 gallons per second.)

As the water in these ancient lakes rose higher than they had ever been before, they began flowing over the top of the moraine down at today's Verrazzano Narrows. That glacial dam melted like butter, releasing a devastating surge of water from the valley that tore across the exposed continental shelf, finally dumping into the sea beyond. As the water rushed out of the valley, eroding the Hudson River Valley further and draining the lakes, it left the delta at Croton Point high and dry.

Knowing that part of Croton Point is a sandy delta helps explain various other phenomena on this spit of land. From today's Croton Point Park

Delta beach facing Haverstraw Bay. Note the sand in contrast to the boulder-strewn beaches elsewhere on the point. *Photo by Scott Craven.*

CROTON POINT SAND

Originally an impediment to the east shore railroad (today's MTA Hudson Line), this sand was excavated to make way for the rails and became a commodity, sold as fill up and down the river. As late as the 1930s, a map showed sand being carted away by barge. In fact, the next time you're walking on the west side of Manhattan, know that you just might be walking on old Croton Point sand.

Beach, one can walk east along the shore back toward Croton and look at the steep slope of the delta. If we could clear away all the vegetation, we would see a cross section of sloping sedimentary layers. These mark the foreset, or what had been the forward-growing face of the delta.

The sand here tells a glacial-era story as well. This is not sand that has been trucked here to maintain a soft, white beach, but rather is left over from the glaciers. Twenty-five thousand years ago, the sand carried out from the mouth of the Croton River was effectively sorted by weight and size into uniform granular consistency, with the coarser sand being deposited here and the fine, silty, clay traveling farther out into the ancient lake.

THE VALLEY: THE CLOVEN DELTA

When it was first formed, the delta extended continuously farther into the river, but it was dissected (or cloven) and a large chunk is missing in the middle. There was a vestigial remnant that was called Money Hill where the admissions booth is now, but in 1924, it was removed and used as fill for the new park road over the swamp.

About eight thousand years ago, the valley between the two sections of delta would begin to play host to a salt marsh as the sea levels rose and flooded the lower portions of the Hudson River. This marsh would exist until the landfill covered it. However, you can still see remnants of it on the south side of the point.

But up until 1924, if you parked your Model T Ford on the narrow strand of sand (a tombolo) that connected Croton Neck to Croton Point and stood on the hood facing south, you could have looked over the marsh and seen

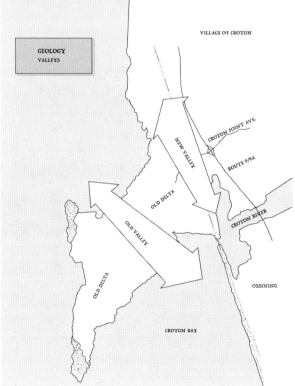

GEOLOGY
VALLEYS

VILLAGE OF CROTON

NEW VALLEY

CROTON POINT AVE.

ROUTE 9/9A

OLD DELTA

OLD VALLEY

CROTON RIVER

OLD DELTA

OSSINING

CROTON BAY

Above: Looking north over the old marsh, circa 1920. Money Hill is on left. *Croton Historical Society.*

Left: Sketch map of the valleys. "New Valley" is man-made, excavated for railroad. "Old Valley" is naturally occurring, now the site of a capped landfill. *Map by Harrison Isaac.*

The landfill today—a man-made one-hundred-foot-tall hill, capped and mitigated. *Photo by Scott Craven.*

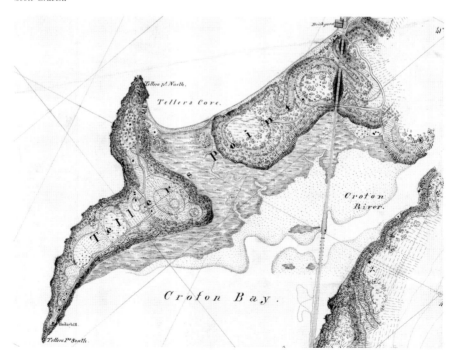

An 1854 U.S. Coastal Survey map. Note the valley that "dissects" the old exposed delta. *Marc Cheshire/NOAA.*

the Ossining waterfront in the distance. Today, all you can see is the looming bulk of the landfill.

The 1854 U.S. Coastal Survey map shows very clearly how the delta was cloven in two by the thundering, ancient Croton River. It gives a nice snapshot of what Croton Point looked like originally, before too much of the sandy delta was mined and before the twentieth-century dump filled in the valley. It's hard to imagine this topography today, and it's a graphic example of how much humans can shape their physical environment.

ENOCH'S POINT: VARVED CLAYS, UNCONSOLIDATED TILL AND A DRUMLIN

This part of the delta was farthest from the mouth of the river and is composed of even finer grained sediments, such as clay and silt. But again, the hand of industry has radically altered the landscape of the point here, and the uneven ground and altered shoreline are evidence of the brickyards that excavated and occupied this area in the nineteenth and twentieth centuries.

Still, along the river's edge, one can occasionally see a cross section of fine sediment with contrasting bars of light and dark layers—these are the varved clays. Deposited in the ancient lake seasonally, you can see the passing of the years marked in these alternating bands (with dark bands deposited in the winter and lighter bands in the summer). Sometimes these bands are separated like sheets of paper, and if you get close enough, you'll find that they have a unique, primeval smell. That's a whiff of the ice age for you.

One of the interesting natural artifacts that can still be recovered on Croton Point today are "clay babies"—small, hardened globs of clay. Formed by silt accreting around a small piece of organic matter (think of a pearl forming around a piece of sand in an oyster), these little clay balls take odd shapes and sometimes even look like little babies. Strangely fascinating, they have entranced people on the point for thousands of years, and some have even been found in ancient living sites. The Nature Center on Enoch's Point has a great collection of clay babies on view.

If one were to visit this Nature Center on the northern point of the park, you would see more curiosities that can confuse the amateur geologist. For example, in front of the Nature Center building, there are large whitish pieces of cut stone. Clearly these were not brought here by the glacier or the river—these stones were transported in the nineteenth century by workers building a mansion on the southern tip of the point. Commonly called Sing

Above: Example of clay varve. *Photo by Scott Craven.*

Right: A "clay baby." *LAB, Lower Hudson Chapter NYSAA; photo by Scott Craven.*

Sing Marble, these blocks of rock are actually dolomitic marble, hand-quarried by inmates across Croton Bay at Sing Sing Prison.

But if you walk behind the Nature Center down to the water, there you will find a beach strewn with boulders of all shapes, sizes and colors that *were* brought here by the glaciers. The difference between this beach and the sandy swimming beach is striking—a very different geological mechanism formed this one.

Geologists have long known that this shoreline, as well as part of the elevated southern point (Teller's Point), is composed of unconsolidated till, or material that was scraped up and then deposited some distance away by the slow-moving glacial ice.

Boulder-strewn beach on Enoch's Point. *Photo by Scott Craven.*

In 1990, Dr. Charles Mergurian and Dr. John E. Sanders of Hoftstra University identified this portion of the shoreline as a drumlin by noting at least three different layers of till along this ridge. The first layer to be deposited, the gray granite boulders, came from the Peekskill area. The second layer, reddish sandstone, came from the old Triassic Haverstraw delta across the river. The third layer, and the most recently deposited, again comes from Peekskill, probably indicating three separate glacial events.

These three layers were then likely shaped by the last glacier to deposit till. As it's an unusual formation to find this far south, Drs. Mergurian and Sanders make a compelling argument as to why it is a drumlin.

TELLER'S POINT: MORE OF THE DRUMLIN, A BOULDER REEF AND VIEWS OF ROCKLAND QUARRY FACES

Shifting focus, let's look at the extreme southern portion of Croton Point: Teller's Point. Here we see the downstream tapering side of the old drumlin. Extending farther downriver is a long boulder reef that extends south and then curls into Croton Bay. As dramatic as it is dangerous to anybody venturing into the water, this submerged feature, only visible

Right: Teller's Point Reef.
Photo by Caroline Curvan.

Below: Trap rock quarry
face across from Croton
Point. *Photo by Scott Craven.*

during extremely low tides, can create strong currents and is constantly shifting and changing.

From Teller's Point, the sweeping curve of the Hudson is framed on the far side of the river by a seemingly continuous ridge with intermittent exposed faces of rock. Although this is part of the same formation that created the iconic Palisades farther downriver, these raw rock faces north of Nyack are largely man-made.

Even so, know that the rocks across the river were created during the Triassic Period, long before Croton Point was formed. With red sandstone deposited like a layer cake in sedimentary beds, an intrusion of magma came up from below, insinuating itself between the layers and cooling into a hard rock called diabase. This diabase would eventually be exposed, and the long vertical columns that formed in it while it was cooling would remind people of stakes, earning the formation its name, the Palisades.

This hard (or "trap") rock would be found to be perfect for gravel. With the paving of roads after the Civil War and the need for ballast for the expanding rail system, the crushed rock from these iconic cliffs would be in great demand. So, the raw quarry faces you see across the river bear silent witness to the extractive Hudson Valley industries of the nineteenth and twentieth centuries.

Now, armed with some visual cues and a sturdy pair of shoes, if we visit Croton Point, we will see millions of years of geology all around us. Architects can look at a building and enjoy it for its aesthetics. But hand those same architects a set of blueprints and now they look at the structure with different eyes. They see the framing, the wiring and the pitch of the roof and appreciate the engineering behind the final form.

Now that we have the "blueprints" to the point, we can do more than just appreciate the sweeping lines of the point's beaches and its odd anvil shape. We can begin to understand the massive forces that shaped the point, and by doing so, we begin to understand the formation of entire Hudson Valley in a more complete and nuanced way.

———◇◆◇———

CROTON POINT LANDFORM CHRONOLOGY
Note: Current convention uses Before Present (BP) dates until you reach the European Contact Period (circa 1500s), and then dates are written as AD (Anno Domini).

2,000,000–25,000 BP
A series of glaciers enlarge and further shape what is today the Hudson Valley.

Circa 25,000 BP
Croton Point begins forming.

Circa 13,700 BP
Glacial Lake Iroquois floods catastrophically down the Hudson Valley, and Croton Point starts taking its current shape.

8,000–6,000 BP
As the climate warms, ice sheets continue to melt, raising global sea levels. The ocean floods the lower portion of the Hudson River, allowing oysters to flourish in its now brackish waters.

AD 1830
Brick companies begin excavating the clay that had formed on the bottom of the old glacial lake.

1846
A valley on the eastern side of the point is cut to allow for the passage of the new East Shore Railroad (today's Metro-North) being built from New York City to Albany.

1923
Westchester County acquires Croton Point and starts a municipal dump in the northeastern corner that will eventually fill in the wetlands.

———◇◆◇———

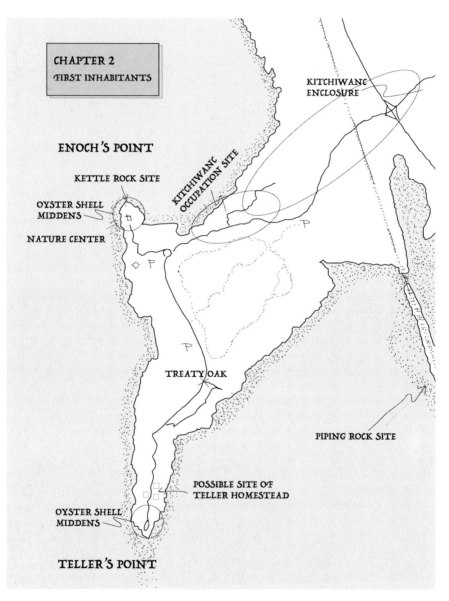

CHAPTER 2
FIRST INHABITANTS

KITCHIWANC
ENCLOSURE

ENOCH'S POINT

KETTLE ROCK SITE

KITCHIWANC
OCCUPATION SITE

OYSTER SHELL
MIDDENS

NATURE CENTER

TREATY OAK

PIPING ROCK SITE

POSSIBLE SITE OF
TELLER HOMESTEAD

OYSTER SHELL
MIDDENS

TELLER'S POINT

Sketch map of Indigenous sites. *Map by Harrison Isaac.*

Chapter 2

THE FIRST PEOPLE

Croton Point has been inhabited since the very first humans followed the retreating glaciers and settled in the Hudson Valley. The Nature Center on Croton Point has a remarkable array of Indigenous artifacts on display, and through them you can get a glimpse into the vibrant communities that lived and prospered on Croton Point for thousands of years before European explorers arrived. One can also peek through the trees and stand on the same rocky shore and see almost the same view that an Archaic person would have seen.

One of the oldest and most obvious places to see evidence of Indigenous occupation on Croton Point is on Enoch's Point. Walking down the path behind the Nature Center, you will find yourself crunching over little white flecks. If you look closely, you will see that they are oyster shells. These shells seem to be piled several feet deep and mixed in with dirt. Trees even grow out of the piles, highlighting their depth and density.

It's a mystery, for there are too many oyster shells for birds or other animals to have left and certainly far too high above the water to have washed up in a storm. How did they all get here?

This is one of the oldest shell heaps (sometimes called "middens") on the north Atlantic coast, begun at least five thousand years ago by Archaic people who used this site seasonally, or at least harvested oysters here seasonally. (Archaeologists can actually identify in what season an oyster was harvested by observing its shell rings, comparable to dating the age of a tree by its tree rings. While not many at Croton Point have been so analyzed, combining

View from Enoch's Point looking across to Haverstraw. *Photo by Scott Craven.*

Remains of ancient shell midden, left by Archaic inhabitants of Croton Point. *Photo by Scott Craven.*

> The Lenapes called the trail up Manhattan Island to Albany *Wickquasgeck*.
>
> The Dutch called it *Brede Weg*.
>
> Today, we call it Broadway, or Route 9.

information from Croton Point and other nearby sites seem to show that many oysters were gathered and eaten in the summer and early fall.)

Despite the fact that Croton Point has been heavily affected by industry and development starting in the 1700s, enough artifacts have still been found to give us a good idea about what the Indigenous people did and how they lived in this area before the arrival of Europeans. The shell middens, both under your feet and nearby, provide rich evidence of Indigenous inhabitation on both sides of the mouth of the Croton River.

Croton Point has long been a popular location, as it is uniquely situated at the rich confluence of the Hudson and Croton Rivers and near to an ancient trail that wound its way from the southern tip of Manhattan Island all the way up to what is now Albany. Any people who lived here would have had access to fresh water, plentiful and varied food and transportation, both up and down the Hudson River and into the interior via the Croton River, for hunting, gathering and eventually agricultural purposes.

Let's put it all into perspective and take a quick look at the big picture before we zero back in on Croton Point.

WHEN DID HUMANS FIRST ARRIVE IN THE HUDSON VALLEY?

Current thinking is that humans began to enter the Hudson Valley region between fourteen thousand and ten thousand years ago, following the Wisconsin ice sheets as they receded north.

The Indigenous populations were gradually displaced by Europeans, who were first documented in the Hudson River in 1524, with Giovanni da Verrazzano's discovery of what is today called the Verrazzano Narrows, located between Brooklyn and Staten Island.

The first European colonists to arrive began writing down their experiences with the people they encountered. And on Croton Point and in the immediate surrounding areas, the historical evidence of Indigenous Lenape people and their ancestors is very present in the form of lithic materials and other tangible

- "Absolute dating" techniques include radiocarbon (C14), thermoluminescence (measuring the ionizing radiation in heated, crystalized materials such as pottery) and dendrochronological techniques (simply, dating by counting tree rings).

- "Relative dating" involves what archaeologists call "stratigraphic position," or how far down they had to dig to find an artifact and what else is found around it, such as animal bones, shells and other artifacts.

- "Ethnobotanical dating" looks at artifacts containing seeds and pollen, providing insights into the climate and conditions at the time of a location's occupation.

artifacts of day-to-day life—in other words, the arrowheads, tools, animal bones, shells and pottery fragments that have been found over the years.

Archaeologists can squeeze an enormous amount of information out of these artifacts. Using both absolute and relative dating techniques, they can pinpoint the date a site was inhabited and can even know what the climate conditions were at the time using ethnobotanical data.

WHAT IS THE OLDEST EVIDENCE OF HUMAN OCCUPATION FOUND ON CROTON POINT?

While the first archaeological dig we know about took place in 1899 on the plateau area on Croton Neck, in the 1960s the shell middens on Enoch's Point were excavated, revealing what is still the earliest evidence of human occupation on Croton Point..

In the early 1960s, the shell middens on Enoch's Point were excavated and revealed what is still the earliest evidence of human occupation on Croton Point. Amateur archaeologist Louis A. Brennan excavated the oyster shell heaps at what he called the Kettle Rock Site on Enoch's Point. Thanks to the relatively new radiocarbon (C14) dating technology of the time, he was the first person to date the shell middens at about six thousand years old.[3]

Brennan inspired others to join him in excavating similar oyster shell heaps along the lower Hudson River, all the way down to Manhattan and up to Bear Mountain.

WHAT WAS CROTON POINT LIKE
WHEN THE FIRST PEOPLE ARRIVED?

As the sheets of ice began receding, humans followed. At first, these native peoples, called Paleo-Indians by archaeologists, encountered an icy, tundra-like landscape, where now-extinct megafauna such as mammoth, mastodon and giant beaver had roamed, along with moose, elk and caribou—animals no longer native to this region and a testament to the colder climate of the time.

As the land began to recover from the glacial chaos that had weighed it down and scoured it away, small pine forests sprang up, and open grasslands began to dot the region. The climate gradually shifted from wet and cold to warmer and more temperate. In this unforgiving world, population density was probably quite low, and the Paleo-Indians likely relied on hunting and gathering. These were a nomadic people, traveling in small family groups, stopping at temporary camps as they followed their food sources.

Archaeologists have found several Paleo-Indian sites in the area around Croton Point that have turned up stone tools, bone deposits and the charcoal

Interpretation of Paleo-Indian peoples. *New York State Museum Native Peoples Hall Exhibit; photo by Scott Craven.*

Broken base fluted point, circa 10,000 BP, from Piping Rock site. *LAB, Lower Hudson Chapter NYSAA. Photo by Scott Craven.*

remains of campfires. While there is currently no evidence that Paleo-Indians lived on Croton Point, there is at least one site just across the Croton River, called Piping Rock (also excavated by Louis Brennan), where an artifact dating to about ten thousand years ago was found.

But there likely were people living here even before ten thousand years ago. At that time, as the glaciers were in the process of retreating and melting, sea levels were lower than where they are today, and the Hudson River may have been a narrower river. So, sites occupied by Indigenous people then may well have been lost to flooding and are now deeply buried.

As the climate stabilized (around seven thousand years ago), the forests evolved to include more deciduous trees, such as oak and hickory. Population likely increased due to the warmer weather, as well as to the increased food options available. It's at this point that the Hudson probably became a tidal estuary, with brackish water that created the right environment for oysters and other fish to flourish. While Archaic people continued as hunter-gatherers, their diet began to include more varieties of fish, nuts, berries and plants. Based on evidence from many other Archaic sites found in the Hudson Valley, Archaic people seemed to have had larger and more permanent settlement sites, not just small encampments.

By the Late Archaic era, about four thousand years ago, the Indigenous people on Croton Point were making and using tools made from native copper. The evidence for this comes in the form of a copper adze blade found on Teller's Point in the early 1900s. (Similar to an axe blade, an adze was mounted to a handle and used to shape wood.) Now, there are obvious differences between trade copper, which would have come from the

Europeans and been melted and cast, and native copper that was beaten, cold, into form. Any native copper found on and around Croton Point likely came from ancient copper mines in the Lake Superior area.

This is one of the more significant finds on Croton Point, as it indicates a sophisticated society that traveled and traded with others and had developed the techniques to craft such tools.

The evidence of pre-European habitation piles up in the form of continued addition to the oyster heaps, as well as more complex and varied arrowheads, spear points and pottery fragments. In fact, thanks to the clay pits that once dotted the peninsula, evidence of pottery making has been discovered over the years in the form of trenches filled with fragments of earthen vessels and charcoal. These native kilns were likely built and used here over the centuries.

What Did Croton Point Look Like When Henry Hudson Arrived in 1609?

One of the earliest maps we have, a 1656 map of New Netherland by early settler Adrien van der Donck, shows Croton Point as an island sitting almost in the middle of the Hudson River. Even accounting for the difficulties in mapmaking at the time, there is good evidence (in the form of the creek called Tanraken, the extensive salt marsh in the middle of the peninsula and subsequent maps) that at this time, the point might have been almost severed from the mainland.

It also seems that there was some sort of a structure on the point when Hudson sailed by. The first written description of it comes to us from an 1819 letter of Philip van Cortlandt, of the nearby Van Cortlandt Manor. In it, he describes an earthwork that would have been located on the high plateau to your right as you enter the park:

> *There is yet the remains of a Fortified Work of Earth made on my land as you advance toward the point in a commanding situation flanked by a Salt Marsh on one side and a Swamp on the Other and as Evidence of Battles Several graves some of large dementions* [sic] *and Hight* [sic] *was found near the work as well as Stone Harpoons for Points of arrows.*[4]

There are several things to observe here. First, note that Van Cortlandt doesn't use the words *fort* or *palisade*—he only mentions an earthwork.

Second, he describes grave mounds being located there. Third, he notes that arrowheads were found, likely on the surface of the point.

But over the years, Van Cortlandt's observations would be twisted by others—sometimes history seems like one big game of telephone, with each historian elaborating on the ones before and in the process embellishing and misinterpreting data.

In 1848, Van Cortlandt's "Fortified Work of Earth" was being referred to by historian Robert Bolton in his *A History of the County of Westchester* as the "Fort of the Kitchawan, [*sic*] one of the most ancient fortresses south of the highlands."[5]

In 1886, J. Thomas Scharf wrote of this area in his *History of Westchester County* and described "[t]he strongest fortress of any in the country…a heavily palisaded stockade. To overlook and protect the important oyster beds…this fort was erected."[6]

The thing is, we don't seem to have any evidence that there was a fort, or that this area was used for military reasons at all. As best we can tell, as the parks department sign installed in 2005 notes, there was an earthwork there that "may have supported a wooden palisade."

In 1899, Mark K. Harrington, on behalf of the Heye's Foundation and the American Museum of Natural History (AMNH), led the first professional archaeological dig on the point, uncovering evidence of human habitation and the remains of something he called a fort. As he wrote in his notes:

> *A portion of the neck has been plowed, but at the time of this field work in 1899, most of it was virgin ground covered with original growth chestnut stumps and second growth timber and brush. A search through this tangle revealed the unmistakable traces of an old fort. From this we learn that the old fort was at least 1200 feet long and 600 feet in width.…A low embankment nowhere more than 2½ feet high, surrounds the neck, running close to the bluffs on the south side. The best-preserved section of all was the western end, north and west of the road crossing, and here the embankment was continuous and distinct, averaging 7 feet wide…these works were, in all probability, employed as a foundation for palisades.[7]*

He also uncovered a four-foot-deep shell heap, as well as the remains of at least one fireplace hearth.

Today, almost nothing remains of a fort or a palisade or an embankment. In the 120 years since Harrington's investigations, a bungalow colony has been built and demolished on this location, and the entire eastern half of

This location was the site of a Native American earthwork, occupation site and burial place during the Late Woodland Period (1000–1600 A.D.). The earthwork may have supported a wooden palisade, or possibly served for ritual purposes. In 2005, working with MALFA (Material Archives Laboratory for Archaeology), the Westchester County Parks, Recreation and Conservation Board named this location an Archaeological Preserve. Please respect this important historical site.

PARKS
WESTCHESTER COUNTY

Westchester Parks sign. *Photo by Scott Craven.*

the plateau has been excavated and carted away for landfill. So, any hint of whatever was here has long been swept clean.

Whether or not Croton Point served any sort of military purpose, all the evidence uncovered shows that this was a vibrant home to Indigenous people. And natural to a place that housed people from their birth to death, burial was a practice present in the area. As recorded in Harrington's notes, there were at least twelve burial mounds within the confines of the plateau, dated to around the 1600s, or the contact period.

Harrington took the remains and burial objects back to the AMNH, and it wasn't until almost one hundred years later that the repatriation process was begun. Some Indigenous people today feel that "Harrington's 'dig' was, in reality, grave robbery and nowhere in the realm of scientific discovery."[8]

Today, this type of excavation is severely restricted, due to the 1990 Native American Graves Protection and Repatriation Act (NAGPRA). Currently, the Lenape (Delaware) Tribe and Nation and Stockbridge-Munsee Nation, among others, continue efforts to repatriate and rebury ancestors and protect burial grounds through this legislation.

Let's take a moment here to honor these ancestors whose final resting places were disturbed.

OTHER ARCHAEOLOGICAL EXCAVATIONS

In the years after Harrington's excavations, others such as James Owens, Alanson Skinner, J. Howard Quimby and Dr. Mary Butler did fieldwork on Croton Point, adding to the collection of artifacts and to the story of the Indigenous communities that called this peninsula home.

Artifacts from these digs—ranging from arrowheads to knives, fishing net sinkers and scraps of pottery—are stored at the Croton Point Nature Center, as well as in the New York State Museum.

In the 1980s, Teller's Point, on the southern end of the peninsula, was excavated, and the findings there helped create an even more specific timeline for Indigenous life on Croton Point. While Louis Brennan's Kettle Rock Site on Enoch's Point mostly just seemed to contain oyster shells, Teller's Point yielded a cornucopia of arrowheads, pottery and animal bone mixed in with the shells. Lead archaeologist Stuart Fiedel noted, "The diversity of materials suggests that a variety of activities took place on Teller's Point, whereas at Kettle Rock, the sole activity seems to have been the processing of oysters."[9]

POST-CONTACT INHABITANTS OF CROTON POINT

The people living on Croton Point in the seventeenth century were known as the Kitchawancs, an Algonquian-speaking people who were culturally and ethnically related to the Wappingers, Munsees, Delawares and Mohicans. Much of what we know of them today comes through the lens of the Europeans who encountered and wrote about them.

One of the very first European accounts to document the Indigenous people of the Hudson Valley comes from Henry Hudson's first mate, Robert Juet. According to Juet's journal, on October 1, 1609, the *Half Moon* anchored at the mouth of the Croton River (then called Kitchawanc by the people who lived there). While Juet doesn't record what specifically happened that night or precisely what he saw on the point, he does describe many other encounters with the people who lived along the river:

> *This day the people of the country came aboard of us, seeming very glad of our coming, and brought green tobacco, and gave us of it for knives and beads. They go in deer skins loose, well dressed. They have yellow copper. They desire clothes, and are very civil....Some [dress] in mantles of feathers, and some in skins of divers sorts of good furs.*[10]

Other contemporaneous European-penned descriptions give us a little more information. In his 1655 book *A History of New Netherland*, Adrien van der Donck wrote that "[b]oth men and women tend to be broad-shouldered and slim-waisted. The hair of the head, before it is changed by old age, is always jet black, quite sleek and uncurled…all, men and women alike, have fine faces with black brown eyes and snow white teeth."[11]

Native people were also often described in such accounts as having tattoos with designs like turtles, serpents, birds or geometric figures, as well as using body paint for war, festivals and mourning.

The lands of the Kitchawancs are believed to have been divided into three areas, each led by a chief called a sachem. One area was Croton Point, the other Verplanck's Point and the third was somewhere in Peekskill (then called Sackoes). The Kitchawancs made up a small portion of the more than thirteen thousand Indigenous people thought to have lived along the Hudson River in 1609.

COLONIZATION

Within five years of Hudson's voyage, the Dutch had established fur-trading posts along the Hudson River and called it all New Netherland. By 1621, the Dutch West India Company (DWIC) had been formed to operate its growing and prosperous fur trade. New Amsterdam, located on the southern tip of Manhattan Island, was designated as the capital of this trading colony.

By 1624, the Dutch were consciously trying to colonize the area by purchasing land from the Indigenous people living there and encouraging European settlers to come to this New World to start new lives and work for the DWIC.

Unsurprisingly, the relationship between the Dutch and the native inhabitants quickly became contentious. The Dutch wanted land and pursued a strategy of "buying" large swaths of land from the people already living on it. The land agreements were inequitable, at best, and represented vastly different cultural understandings.

According to the resource guide of the Stockbridge-Munsee Band of Mohican Indians, Sachem John Waunaucon Quinney addressed this in a speech given in 1854:

> *Nothing that deserved the name of purchase was made….The Indians were informed, in many instances, that they were selling one piece of land when*

they were conveying another and much larger limits. Should a particular band, for purposes of hunting or fishing, for a time leave its usual place of residence, the land was said to be abandoned, and the Indian claim extinguished. To legalize and confirm titles thus acquired, laws and edicts were subsequently passed, and these laws were said then to be, and are now called, justice.[12]

The consequence of this aggressive land acquisition by Europeans was that hunting grounds were destroyed, native farms were uprooted and the wildly lucrative beaver was trapped and hunted into near extinction. Misunderstandings and violence pitted the two sides against each other.

By 1639, it was "forbidden to sell guns, powder or lead to the Indians, on pain of being punished by death."[13] Willem Kieft, the director of the DWIC, was particularly harsh, levying taxes on the Lenape people, demanding payments in maize, wampum or furs. The Lenapes bitterly opposed these payments, considering them unjust forms of taxation that ignored their sovereignty and independence.

In response to Kieft's mandates, the Lenapes began attacking Dutch settlements. Violence between the two groups became more vicious and frequent, escalating into the brutal "Kieft's War," which was waged until 1645. (It was during this violent interlude that one of the original Massachusetts Bay Colony settlers, Anne Hutchinson and her family, were killed in what is today's Pelham. She is mostly remembered by the parkway in lower Westchester County that bears her name.)

In retaliation, the Dutch militia intensified the violence by destroying Indian villages and engaging in the indiscriminate slaughter of native people—warriors, women and children alike. After the Bedford Massacre in February 1644, where Captain John Underhill (ancestor of the Underhills who would purchase Croton Point in the 1800s) led a group that slaughtered an estimated seven hundred of the Siwanoy and Wechquaesgeek bands, the Indian nations saw no other option but to sign a treaty to stop the violence. In August 1645, "a firm and inviolable peace"[14] was signed.

It is this treaty that was memorialized on Croton Point in 1960 by the New York State Society of the Children of the American Revolution. The plaque placed there, near the RV park entrance, purportedly indicates the site of the treaty signing under what was called Treaty Oak, stating, "At this site stood a magnificent oak tree under which, according to tradition, in A.D. 1645 Aepjen, Chief Sachem of the Mohegans, signed a Treaty of Peace with the Dutch on behalf of the Kitchiwanghs."

WILLIAM AND SARAH TELLER ON CROTON POINT

Interestingly, the various histories written about Westchester County all note that around this time, a William and Sarah Teller received permission from the Kitchawancs to run a trading post on Croton Point. This even appears today on the Westchester County Parks website.

Yet there is no record of a William and Sarah Teller in the Teller family tree around 1660. There was, however, a William Teller whose mother-in-law was named Sarah Kierstede and whose second husband was Cornelius van Bursum.

This was likely Sarah Roeleff Kierstede van Bursum Stouthoff (1626–1693). She was the daughter of early Dutch landowner Roeloff Jansen, and she married three times. She was "said to have been more proficient in the Indian language than any other person in the colony" and served as the interpreter for the 1664 treaty negotiations between Peter Stuyvesant and the Indians. Because of her service, "she was presented with a large tract of land on the west side of the North River, by Oritany, the chief of the Hackinsack and Tappan Indians."*

Given the fact that Teller's Point was sometimes called Sarah's Point on old maps, Sarah's relative fame for a woman of her time and an 1816 letter written by Philip van Cortlandt discussing the Tellers' trading post, it's easy to see how this legend could have been perpetuated.

* Brodhead, *History of the State of New York*, 731.

However, this likely was not the actual site of the treaty signing, as no records of such an event have ever been found. (The plaque states that it is only "according to tradition" that a treaty signing took place there.) John Phillips of the Croton Point Nature Center suggests that "soon after the treaty was signed in New Amsterdam, the Kitchawanc held a ceremony under an oak at Croton Point affirming the New Amsterdam event, perhaps attended by Sachem Aepjen during his return from Fort Amsterdam to the Mahican territories."

Just about twenty years later, in 1664, the English sailed three ships into New York Harbor and demanded that the Dutch surrender. They did, and just like that, New Amsterdam became an English colony, renamed New York. But things went from bad to worse for the Kitchawancs, as their removal from the area they called Lenapehoking was continued by the British.

In 1682, Croton Point would appear again in European documents, when the first recorded purchase of Croton Point land occurred between Cornelius van Bursum and twenty Indigenous people. According to the deeds held in the files of the Westchester County Archives, on February 4, 1682, Van Bursum purchased the following real estate:

> *All that parcel* [sic], *neck, or point of Land, with the Marsh, Meadow ground, or valley thereto Adjoining and Belonging, Situate lying and being on the east side of the North or Hudson's River…commonly called and known by the name of Slauper's Haven, and by the Indians Navish, the Meadow being called by the Indians Senasqua, being bounded by the said river and a certain creek called or known to the Indians by the name of Tanrackan, and divided from the Main land by certain trees marked by the Indians, together with half of said Creek &c. for, and in consideration of a certain sum of Wampum, and divers other goods, paid by Cornelius van Bursum.*[15]

LENAPES TODAY

What happened to the Kitchawancs after the loss of their homelands to European colonization? Many moved to the Berkshires and became known as the "Stockbridge Munsees"; they survived by living in a missionary settlement in Stockbridge, Massachusetts. This nation endured repeated removals throughout the eighteenth and nineteenth centuries. Today, they live in in Bowler, Wisconsin, as the Stockbridge-Munsee Community. Other Lenape people also continue to exist as sovereign nations in Oklahoma and Ontario, Canada. Despite having been removed from their original lands, throughout the nineteenth century, the Kitchawancs and other Indigenous people would return to Croton Point for an autumnal oyster festival they called *kintecays*.

Today, the Lenape Nation and the Stockbridge-Munsee Nation, among others, continue to honor their ancestors and strengthen the connection with their homeland through repatriation, culture and language education.

———◇✳◇———

FIRST PEOPLE CHRONOLOGY

Note: Current convention uses Before Present (BP) dates until you reach the Contact Period (circa 1500s) and then dates are written as AD (Anno Domini).

12,000–10,000 BP (Paleo-Indian Period)

Final retreat of glaciers. First appearance of native peoples in the Hudson Valley, as nomadic hunter/gatherers. No evidence of Paleo-Indian habitation on Croton Point, although nearby archaeological sites have found Paleo-Indian artifacts.

10,000 BP–3,000 BP (Archaic Periods, including Early, Middle and Late)

Transformation into more sophisticated and settled society. Archaic artifacts have been found almost everywhere on the point.

3,000 BP–400 BP (Transitional and Woodland Periods, includes Early, Middle and Late)

Pottery, evidence of agriculture and ritual burials—all seen and documented on Croton Point.

AD 1524 (Contact Period)

Europeans arrive in the Hudson Valley: Giovanni da Verrazzano in 1524, Henry Hudson in 1609 and others.

1645

In treaty with the Dutch, Sachem Aepjen negotiates use of land by Kitchawanc (a subgroup of Munsee Lenapes).

1682

Land agreement between Cornelius Van Bursum and Kitchawancs.

———◇✳◇———

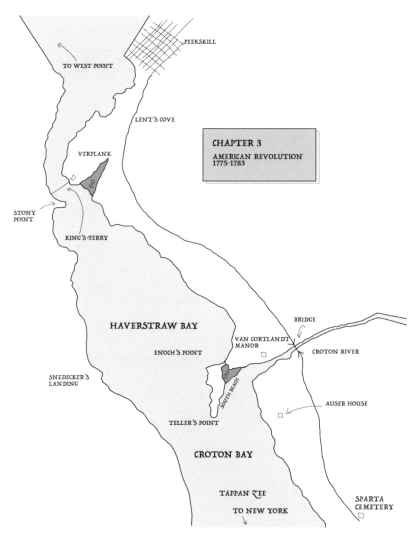

PEEKSKILL

TO WEST POINT

LENT'S COVE

VERPLANK

STONY
POINT

KING'S FERRY

CHAPTER 3

AMERICAN REVOLUTION
1775-1783

HAVERSTRAW BAY

ENOCH'S POINT

SNEDECKER'S
LANDING

TELLER'S POINT

CROTON BAY

TAPPAN ZEE

TO NEW YORK

BRIDGE

VAN CORTLANDT
MANOR

CROTON RIVER

SOUTH BEACH

AUSER HOUSE

SPARTA
CEMETERY

Sketch map of Revolutionary War sites on and around Croton Point. *Map by Harrison Isaac.*

Chapter 3

THE AMERICAN REVOLUTION

The importance of the North River in the present contest and the necessity of defending it, are subjects which have been so frequently and so fully discussed, and are so well understood, that it is unnecessary to enlarge upon them.
—*December 2, 1777 letter from George Washington to General Putnam*

The real Revolution was so troubling and strange that once the struggle was over, a generation did its best to remove all trace of the truth. No one wanted to remember how after boldly declaring independence they quickly lost their way; how patriotic zeal had lapsed into cynicism and self-interest; and how, just when all seemed lost, a traitor saved them from themselves
—Valiant Ambition, *Nathaniel Philbrick*

From 1775 to 1783, the conflict known as the American Revolution swirled around Croton Point, which stood as a mostly silent witness to massive military expeditions up and down the river. The British military's primary objective was to divide the colonies by controlling the full length of the Hudson River to put down this uprising. The Americans were equally determined to stop them.

The choke point was just a few miles north of Croton Point at King's Ferry. Overlooking Haverstraw Bay, Enoch's Point offers a clear view north to Stony and Verplanck's Points. The stretch of water between the two is King's Ferry. With the English controlling New York City for the majority of the war, this simple crossing took on huge strategic and tactical significance. North of it, the river is narrow, but access is difficult because of the high, rocky shores. South of it, the river is tremendously wide and was dangerously close to the English fleet in New York Harbor.

From 1777 to 1780, King's Ferry was the site of several battles and skirmishes. The British were able to capture it, taking Fort Montgomery in October 1777, where they were able to cut the chain that obstructed the Hudson and get as far north as Kingston.

Standing on Croton Point then, you would have seen the British warships and troop-carrying barges passing by. You would have heard the booms and the flashes of the cannons. You might even have seen General Washington ride by on the Post Road with his entourage. However, sitting on the edge of the Neutral Ground, Croton Point would have been untouched by battle. At most, the peninsula was used by both the British and the Americans for foraging expeditions and as a troop landing site.

However, on September 20, 1780, the actions of two young Patriots on Croton Point changed the course of history.

Five years into the Revolution, the British were struggling. France had come into the war on the side of the Americans, and the war in the South was going poorly for the British. General Henry Clinton was still occupying New York City, but it was becoming apparent that the British strategy of minor attacks throughout the region was not going to draw General Washington's army out of the Highlands into a major battle. It was in this stalemate that Benedict Arnold found opportunity.

To this day, his name is one of the more recognizable ones from the Revolutionary War. While we may not all remember the details of his actions, we all know that his name is synonymous with treason.

Until September 1780, George Washington thought of Benedict Arnold as one of the most reliable officers in the Continental army. Combining daring, skill and audacity, Arnold notched up significant triumphs over the British in battles such as Fort Ticonderoga, Saratoga and Ridgefield. He was badly wounded several times—in one battle, he had two horses shot out from under him in as many days. And he was permanently disabled from a musket ball that had shattered his leg at the Battle of Saratoga, causing him immense pain for the rest of his life.[16] At one point, John Adams even suggested that the Continental Congress create a medal in Arnold's honor to acknowledge his bravery and sacrifices for the Patriot cause.

But Arnold's personality contained an arrogance that caused him to keenly feel any perceived slight or lack of respect, and he became increasingly

THE NEUTRAL GROUND

Once the British took New York City in the fall of 1776, General Washington and his Continental army retreated north. A thirty-mile strip along the Hudson from the Bronx to the south bank of the Croton River was considered part of the Neutral Ground, and no formal battles were fought here. For much of the Revolutionary War, this area found itself between two competing and hungry armies. Forces from both sides would sally forth into the Neutral Ground looking for food, provisions and subjects not sympathetic with their cause. It became a territory of raids, checkpoints and ambush where atrocities were committed by all.

bitter as the war progressed, feeling that he should have been promoted to the rank of general more quickly. Dogging his career were ongoing rumblings of war profiteering, the proceeds of which he allegedly used to finance his wildly extravagant lifestyle.

In June 1779, the allegations of corruption caught up with him, and a court-martial was begun. In January 1780, Arnold was acquitted of all but two of the most minor charges. His punishment, it seems, was simply a strongly worded letter from the Court Martial Board expressing its disappointment in Benedict's "imprudent and improper" actions.[17] However, Washington went on to give Arnold command of West Point. Despite this, by July 1780, Arnold was negotiating with the British to hand over classified military information, hoping to give them the key to the Hudson River Valley.

West Point, which was just a small fort then and not the famed military academy it is today, was seen as key to the British strategy of splitting the colonies and ending this troublesome revolution. For several months, resentful at not being promoted after his actions at Saratoga and juggling his creditors, Arnold had been secretly corresponding with Major John André, head of the British Secret Service in America and adjutant to General Henry Clinton, hatching a plot to turn West Point over to the British. (It should be mentioned here that Major André had briefly courted Arnold's young, Loyalist second wife, the lovely Peggy Shippen, and continued corresponding with her after she married Arnold. She seems to have played a major role in connecting the two men.)

Right: Colonel
Benedict Arnold
in 1776. *Portrait by
Thomas Hart (public
domain).*

Opposite: View of
Snedeker's Landing
today from Croton
Point. *Photo by Scott
Craven.*

Arnold had insisted on writing to André in code and using *noms de
guerre*—Arnold was "Gustavus" and André was "John Anderson." Because
of the uncertainty as to Gustavus's actual identity, General Clinton insisted
that Major André have a face-to-face meeting with this mysterious double
agent before any deal was finalized. Here is where Croton Point takes
center stage, although the details of the story are hard to pin down.

It begins with the British sloop of war HMS *Vulture*, a well-known sight
along the Hudson, as it had been patrolling the waters since the occupation
of New York City in 1776. On the morning of September 20, 1780, John
"Rifle Jack" Peterson and George "Moses" Sherwood spied it anchored off
Croton Point.

There are several stories regarding what brought the HMS *Vulture* to
their attention that day, where Peterson and Sherwood actually were
standing and what sparked the idea that they should take action. Perhaps
on that morning they saw a barge of British soldiers preparing to land on

Croton Point and opened fire. Perhaps they just realized that the *Vulture* was within cannon range of Croton Point.

At some point on the twentieth, Peterson and Sherwood headed off to Fort Lafayette in Verplanck to secure a cannon. And after dark on the night of the twentieth, Major John André was rowed from Dobbs Ferry to board the *Vulture*. André would spend the night on the *Vulture*, writing a letter to finalize his meeting with Arnold the next day.

After nightfall on the twenty-first, Joshua Hett Smith and two oarsmen, commissioned by Arnold, silently rowed up to the *Vulture* to take Major André to the appointed meeting place, called Snedeker's Landing, on the other side of the river near Haverstraw.

Overnight, Major André and Benedict Arnold negotiated the price and logistics of Arnold's treason. For 20,000 British pounds sterling (which is more than $3 million in today's dollars), Arnold would not only give the British the plans to West Point, but also, as its commander, he would make sure that the majority of the fighting men weren't there when the British made their assault. Even worse, George Washington had just indicated his plan to inspect West Point in the coming days, and Arnold was ready to sacrifice Washington as well.

As the night stretched to a close, Joshua Hett Smith became increasingly anxious about the tide and the light and feasibility of rowing André back to the *Vulture* without being seen. Arnold had anticipated that his negotiations would take time and had arrived with two horses. He and André rode them the few miles back to Smith's house and continued negotiating.

Soon after sunrise on the morning of September 22, Peterson and Sherwood returned to Croton Point with a four-pound cannon and began shelling the *Vulture*. According to Shonnard and Spooner's *History of Westchester County*, "a small breastwork was erected at the west end of the Point, the gun planted and a fire directed upon the Vulture which was returned by several broadsides. The Americans fired with effect, shivering some of the spars of the vessel."[18]

At the slack high tide, when the river isn't moving in either direction and with no wind, the *Vulture* was at the mercy of the Americans' gun. All it could do was return fire. Legend has it that "[f]or many years after this great event, Peterson was accustomed to point out to his sons and others one of the cannonballs lodged in an oak tree on Teller's Point which was fired from the Vulture on this occasion."[19] This cannonball was retrieved from this oak tree by Richard Underhill nearly a century later and given to a Dr. George J. Fisher of Ossining. Today, the cannon Peterson and Sherwood may have used is on display outside the Peekskill Museum.

As soon as the tide started to ebb, the *Vulture* cut its anchor cable and dropped rapidly downstream to safety, leaving Major André stranded on the other side of river. Local folklore also holds that on its way downriver, another one of the *Vulture*'s cannonballs pierced a colonial-era red headstone in Ossining's old Sparta Cemetery. This headstone remained intact, with a clear cannonball hole in it, until the 1970s.

As the sloop retreated down the Hudson, back to the British lines, André is said to have watched in horror from an upstairs window in Smith's house, knowing that he was now alone behind enemy lines in his telltale red coat. Arnold, however, was unruffled. He gave André a change of clothes, a pass through the American lines and instructions to hide the plans to West Point in his stockings.

Joshua Hett Smith accompanied André back down to the Neutral Ground, crossing at King's Ferry and riding south. Smith left André at the bridge in Croton then located on Van Cortlandt manor, at the very foot of Croton Point. André continued on alone until he was caught in today's Tarrytown. He was hanged as a spy and buried in Tappan, New York.

Benedict Arnold escaped and led British forces against the Americans for the rest of the war. He and Peggy sailed to England, where, dying in 1801, he was interred in the wall of a minor church in London—wearing, as legend has it, a Continental uniform.

Above: Four-pound cannon, purportedly the one used by Peterson and Sherwood to shell the HMS *Vulture* on September 22, 1780. *Peekskill Historical Society; photo by Scott Craven.*

Left: Headstone at Sparta Cemetery that supposedly was pierced by a cannonball from the HMS *Vulture* in September 1780. *Photo by Scott Craven.*

Standing near the Croton Point Park pavilion today, it's easy to miss the bronze tablet on the boulder just north of the structure. Commissioned by the Daughters of the American Revolution and placed there in 1967 to commemorate their heroic actions, the story of John Peterson and Moses Sherwood has often been glossed over. But we should take as much time on their life story as we did with Arnold, as both men were representative of the gritty heroism of the people who stood up and joined the Revolution.

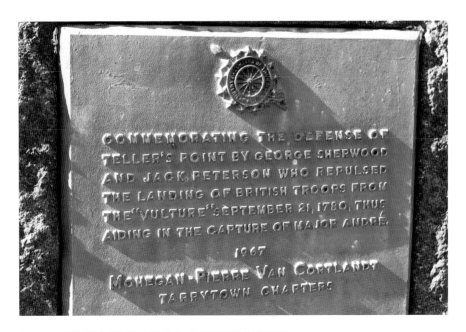

Above: Plaque commemorating John Peterson and Moses Sherwood's heroic actions, installed in 1967 by the Daughters of the American Revolution. *Photo by Scott Craven.*

Left: Grave site of John P. Peterson, Bethel Cemetery, Croton-on-Hudson, New York. *Photo by Ken Sargeant.*

John Peterson was Black and even possibly of Kitchawanc descent. It is not known if he was born into slavery, but various sources indicate that he was raised by a Job Sherwood. According to an 1859 article published in the *Weekly Anglo-African*, Peterson was about the same age and very close to Job's son Isaac, who had enlisted in the Continental army as a lieutenant. Peterson enlisted as a private in the same regiment.

The two saw serious action, and Lieutenant Sherwood reportedly died of wounds at the Battle of Saratoga, with Peterson by his side. "The devoted attachment of Peterson to the gallant and much-lamented Lieutenant was observed by Colonel van Cortlandt who, without solicitation, gave him his discharge from the service to enable him to return home with the effects which belonged to the Lieutenant."[20]

Upon his discharge, Peterson was assigned to the local militia under the command of Colonel James Livingston. Moses Sherwood was also a member of Livingston's militia and very likely related to Job and Isaac Sherwood. As the *Weekly Anglo-African noted*, "It was pure patriotism that led him and Sherwood to attack an enemy of superior numbers and power... [and] thwarted André in his design to embark on board the Vulture with his death warrant of American liberty."[21]

For many years, Peterson lived on the Van Cortlandt Manor in recognition of his service but later had to fight to receive his Revolutionary War pension. He was buried at the Bethel Cemetery in Croton at the age of 103. His brother-in-arms, Moses Sherwood, was buried near the headstone at Sparta Cemetery supposedly pierced by the ball from the *Vulture*.

John Peterson and Moses Sherwood did not know what the *Vulture*'s mission was, but they knew that ship was the enemy. They lived very different realities but acted together, aggressively and courageously, and in doing so created our nation.

THE NEUTRAL GROUND

The beach on the south side of the point is not on any official tourist map and can only be accessed during low tide by bushwhacking through the reeds past the groundskeeper's house or across from the old wine cellars. This stretch of sand is popular with people who frequent the point, as it constantly changes, revealing old pilings, bricks and a variety of seasonal flotsam. Over the years, it has been the scene of schooners loading fruit and flowers, pleasure boats unloading day trippers, seaplanes docking and fishermen hauling in massive nets.

During the Revolution, this beach would have been the dividing line between the American lines and the Neutral Ground. When the war was in its final days, Croton Point came face to face with one of the last violent encounters in this burnt-over Neutral Ground.

A fertile area for tall tales and legends, the Neutral Ground was described at length in James Fenimore Cooper's florid novel *The Spy*. Another work that likely gives a more factual version of this time is the Macdonald Papers, a series of interviews with former soldiers in the early nineteenth century that describe some of the most colorful and despicable characters of the war, as well as experiences in the Neutral Ground.

After the American victory at Yorktown in October 1781, major campaigning stopped and the preparations for the British evacuation of the colonies began. Most forces took this as an opportunity to avoid further conflict, but not those operating in the Neutral Ground. There had been so much bitterness and hatred over the previous eight years that the inevitable end of the war may have been an incentive for some to increase the tempo of operations against each other while they still could.

On January 24, 1783, American captain John Williams and John Odell of the Westchester Guides led a force of fifty soldiers south through the Neutral Ground. They had received information that their nemesis for the last eight years, Lieutenant Colonel James De Lancey, leader of the hated Cowboys, was holed up in his lair in the West Bridge section of what is now the Bronx. Williams and Odell could not pass up this opportunity to surprise De Lancey, their primary target for years, and either kill or capture him. Unfortunately for them, surprise was impossible to achieve, and when they descended on De Lancey's headquarters, they discovered that he had escaped.

As was common in this lawless theater of the conflict, the American raiding party took everything of value, including prisoners and horses. Pursued by De Lancey's Loyalist forces as they fled north, the Americans were compelled to fight a rear-guard action near what is now Yonkers.

Approaching the Croton River, the Americans split up at the crossroads and headed back to their respective homes in northern Westchester. With a false sense of security, having beaten their pursuers back, they felt they could stop south of the river to divide their spoils.

It was here that the British surprised the Americans, pursuing them as they scattered and fled out onto the frozen river. Most were killed or captured, but bursting forth from the deadly scrum was John Odell, on a large dapple-gray horse, pursued by two of De Lancey's mounted troopers.

Croton Bay today, site of one of the final raids in the Neutral Ground near Croton Point. *Photo by Scott Craven.*

Hacking at each other with cutlasses, Odell escaped to the south side of Croton Point, galloping through frozen swampland until he reached the road that would lead him behind the American lines. He survived the war and died in his bed in 1835.

This incident is representative of many of the actions that occurred in the Neutral Ground: an impromptu raid based on information targeting an individual, fueled by the acrimony and hatred that had initiated the War for American Independence.

Today, as you stand on the edge of the Neutral Ground looking south, you can imagine yourself back to that uncertain time in our nation's history, when a few courageous souls took matters into their own hands and changed the course of history.

———◄✖►———

AMERICAN REVOLUTION CHRONOLOGY
1775
First shots of Revolution are fired at Lexington and Concord (April 19).

1776
British defeat Washington in Brooklyn and occupy New York, where they will remain for the next eight years.

1779
British land on Teller's Point to forage for cattle. The entire group, ten men and a Native American guide, is captured by the Americans (February 28).

British land more than one thousand soldiers on Croton Point in preparation to take the King's Ferry between Verplanck and Stony Point (May 31).

British land on Teller's Point and sack the Van Cortlandt Manor House.

1780
Enoch Crosby (American spy made famous by James Fenimore Cooper's novel *The Spy*) is stationed on Croton Point. Luring a barge full of British sailors ashore, he and his men capture them.

American general Benjamin Lincoln departs from Teller's Point with 1,200 men in an unsuccessful attack at the Kings Bridge section of what is now the Bronx (July 2).

Americans John "Rifle Jack" Peterson and George Moses Sherwood fire on the HMS *Vulture*, disrupting Benedict Arnold and British major John André's plan to take West Point (September 20–22).

1783

Americans returning from a raid are surprised in the Neutral Ground in Sing Sing. Fleeing on the ice to Croton Bay, only John Odell escapes via Croton Point (January 8).

Treaty of Paris is signed, ending the American Revolutionary War (September 3).

1952

A four-pound cannon is found in Verplanck, possibly the one used to shell the HMS *Vulture*, and is donated to the Peekskill Historical Society.

1967

The Daughters of the American Revolution place a plaque on Croton Point commemorating the shelling of the *Vulture* by Anderson and Sherwood.

2004

The African American Heritage Trail of Westchester County is created; Croton Point is a featured stop.

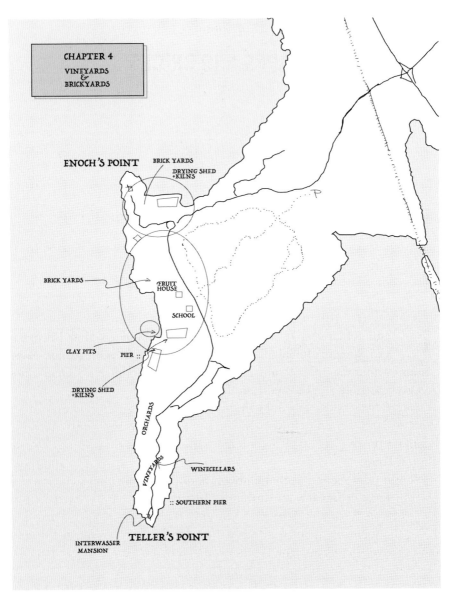

ENOCH'S POINT

BRICK YARDS

DRYING SHED
+KILNS

BRICK YARDS

FRUIT
HOUSE

SCHOOL

CLAY PITS

PIER ::

DRYING SHED
+KILNS

ORCHARDS

VINEYARDS

WINECELLARS

:: SOUTHERN PIER

TELLER'S POINT

INTERWASSER
MANSION

Sketch map of vineyards and brickyards. *Map by Harrison Isaac.*

Chapter 4

GRAPES AND BRICKS

Grapes really are one of the good things in life.[22]
—*Dr. Richard T. Underhill*

L and on Croton Point changed hands many times after Cornelius van Bursum's initial transaction in 1682. For the most part, it stayed within the Teller/Van Cortlandt families, who operated small farms and even possibly a trading post on the point.

By 1697, most of Croton Neck had been incorporated into Stephanus van Cortlandt's Manor. It was also around this time that, legend has it, the infamous pirate Captain William Kidd buried treasure near Money Hill on Croton Point.

Now, it does seem true that Captain Kidd hid pirate plunder in various places—most definitively on Gardiner's Island in about 1699. According to *East Hampton History* by Jeannette Edwards Rattroy, upon Kidd's arrest in 1701, the following items were turned over to the authorities: "Gold dust, bars of silver, pieces of eight, rubies great and small, diamonds, candlesticks, porringers"[23]—exactly what you'd imagine a pirate would hide.

The next significant chapter in the development of Croton Point came in 1804: Thomas Jefferson is president, Alexander Hamilton perishes in his infamous duel with Aaron Burr and Robert Underhill purchases 250 acres on Croton Point.

Captain Kidd's treasure, from the *Crawbucky Tales* by Frank H. Pierson, circa 1920s. *Westchester County Archives.*

VINEYARDS AND ORCHARDS

Underhill and his wife, Mary, lived on the point with their eleven children and a handful of servants. While early maps of the point show several structures scattered about, the consensus is that the Underhills settled in and renovated a house that had likely belonged to the Teller family. Last known as the "Greenberg House" before its demolition in the mid-twentieth century, it stood between today's RV Park and the brick parks department buildings.

Before his Croton Point purchase, Underhill had owned a flour and gristmill nearby on the Croton River with his two brothers, Abraham and Joshua.

Croton Point from above, with Enoch's Point in foreground. *Photo by Brendan Donohue.*

Teller's Point from above, looking south. *Photo by Brendan Donohue.*

Croton Point from Rockland County. *Photo by Scott Craven.*

Looking south from Pavilion (site of old brickyard and clay field). *Photo by Scott Craven.*

Western edge of capped landfill. *Photo by Brendan Donohue.*

Looking north from Pavilion. Note the Peterson and Sherwood plaque on boulder at left. *Photo by Scott Craven.*

Another Underhill brickyard site as seen today. *Photo by Scott Craven.*

Modern Park Pavilion. *Photo by Scott Craven.*

Looking south, with Hook Mountain in the distance. *Photo by Caroline Curvan.*

Looking south to Croton Point from Croton-on-Hudson. *Photo by Scott Craven.*

Looking south to Croton Point from Croton-on-Hudson. Julie Hart de Beers, *Hudson River at Croton Point*, 1869, oil on canvas. *Wikimedia Commons.*

Capped landfill today, from park entrance. *Photo by Scott Craven.*

Grasslands Restoration Area sign. *Photo by Scott Craven.*

"The Croton Dump Operation Is Just a Few Hundred Feet from Croton Point Park." *Photo by Blanche Will, 1972, National Archives.*

Croton Point Park Headquarters. *Photo by Scott Craven.*

Haverstraw Beach, looking west toward Croton-on-Hudson. *Photo by Scott Craven.*

Sanford Robinson Gifford, *Morning in the Hudson, Haverstraw Bay*, 1866, oil on canvas. Terra Foundation for American Art, Daniel J. Terra Collection, 1993.11. *Photography ©Terra Foundation for American Art, Chicago.*

Old Pier, South Beach, looking toward Teller's Point. *Photo by Caroline Curvan.*

Opposite, top: Old Pier, South Beach, looking toward Croton-on-Hudson. *Photo by Caroline Curvan.*

Opposite, bottom: Fallen tree, winter, South Beach. *Photo by Caroline Curvan.*

Right: Trail through *Phragmites*, South Beach. *Photo by Caroline Curvan.*

Below: Brick and fish, South Beach, 2021. *Photo by Caroline Curvan.*

Sunset on South Beach looking toward Teller's Point. *Photo by Scott Craven.*

Bald eagle landing on sandspit off Croton Point. *Photo by Bonnie Coe.*

Above: South Beach looking toward Teller's Point, 1866. Sanford Robinson Gifford, *Hook Mountain, Near Nyack, on the Hudson*, 1866, oil on canvas. Note the cupola of Interwasser peeking up through trees on right side. *Yale University Art Gallery.*

Right: Teller's Point Reef. *Photo by John Curvan.*

Bald eagle off Croton Point. *Photo by Bonnie Coe.*

Immature bald eagle, flying (sometimes called "Dirty Bird"). *Photo by Scott Craven.*

Right: Coyote in winter. *Photo by Bonnie Coe.*

Below: Robert Havell Jr., *View of Hudson from Horton's Road Near Croton*. *Minneapolis Institute of Art*.

Robert Havell Jr., *Hudson River North to Croton Point*, 1851. *Ossining Historical Society.*

Paul Weber, *View of the Hudson River Near Fishkill Creek*. Some say that this is actually a view from the Croton Aqueduct. *New Britain Museum of American Art.*

On Croton Point, Underhill began by farming typical crops of the time—Newtown Pippin apples and castor beans are often mentioned. However, he quickly pivoted and began raising watermelon to take advantage of the supply chain disruption due to the War of 1812, when the British naval blockade made it difficult to export anything along the Atlantic coast. It is said that as many as six boats at a time would anchor off Croton Point waiting to transport shipments of Underhill's fruit.

In 1827, despite his Quaker background, Robert Underhill began experimenting with grape growing and winemaking. He met with little success because he was trying to cultivate European varieties that were not suited to the climate.

When Robert Underhill died in 1829, two of his sons, Richard and William, acquired the land. Richard got the 85 acres containing the vineyards and orchards on the southern side, as well as the tip of Teller's Point, and William took over 165 acres on the northern side of the peninsula, rich with clay deposits.

Dr. Richard T. Underhill had trained as a medical doctor but stopped regular practice after inheriting his Croton Point land, apparently preferring to turn his father's orchards and vineyards into award-winning and money-

MONEY HILL

In the 1920s, local Ossining reporter Frank H. Pierson wrote and illustrated many fanciful stories in his *Crawbucky Tales* about evidence of Captain Kidd's treasure on Croton Point and the "Satanic forces" that protected it. The belief in the burial of Captain Kidd's gold on Croton Point persisted well into the twentieth century. In fact, in 1924, when Westchester County wanted to reroute the road leading into its new park, it called for contractors to bid on the removal of Money Hill. While we don't know exactly why Money Hill got that name, a remarkable forty-seven bids were received for the job. And it was even written into the contract that if "any relics or treasures are found, they will become the property of the Parks Commission."* As far as we know, nothing was found.

* *Scarsdale Inquirer*, "Revives Tradition of Captain Kidd's Famous Buried Treasure," 1.

making enterprises. He began planting Catawba and Isabella grapes, which were far hardier and disease-resistant than those his father had started.

Underhill's vineyard may well have been the first commercial vineyard in the northeast. Eventually covering about fifty acres on Teller's Point, it sported rows of vines about six to eight feet apart that ultimately featured a variety of hardy grapes that produced a sweet wine of "therapeutic value."[24]

There's a delightfully detailed description of Underhill's vineyards and orchards in Alden Spooner's manual, *Upon American and Foreign Grapevines.* Amusingly, Spooner notes that he sold ten thousand cuttings of Isabella grapes to Richard's brother William Underhill in 1832 for cultivation. But, says Spooner, "as Dr. R.T. Underhill is a very intelligent and successful cultivator, I shall notice him and his vineyard hereafter."

In 1843, Spooner made an excursion out to Croton Point from New York City. Despite the day being "very tempestuous and wet," he was given a thorough tour of Dr. Underhill's orchards and vineyards. Several pages are spent discussing the minutiae of soil amendments, methods of trimming the vines and the supports and wires used, with Mr. Spooner being quite impressed with Underhill's approach, concluding that the Croton Point vineyards were "such a sight as probably was not to be seen elsewhere in America."[25]

He also describes "a long artificial pond parallel to the shore…which had been made by taking out many thousands loads of peat or muck which had been carried to the vineyard on the high ground in its natural state.…The

COMMODORE VANDERBILT AND THE UNDERHILL MILL

Cornelius Vanderbilt, who would become one of the richest Americans at the time in the domains of shipping and railroads, began his career as the captain of small sailboats, occasionally ferrying freight up and down the Hudson. Frederick Underhill maintains that Vanderbilt regularly stopped at the Underhill Mill on the Croton River to deliver grain and pick up flour to take to Manhattan. At the time, the Croton River was deep enough to allow passage for periaugers—small, two-masted sailing ships. Today, due to the 1841 flood caused by the bursting of the first Croton Dam, the mouth of the Croton is filled with sediment and is only navigable by kayaks or canoes.

pond had been thus made by excavation to the depth of 10 feet and had become a valuable fishpond."[26]

This fishpond on the south beach, which no longer exists, was also noted in a *New York Times* article as "The Plum Tree Lake." While "the choicest fish, as yellow and Croton-striped bass, white perch and sunfish" were mentioned in passing, "the main feature of this lake is, however, its complete border of plum trees, so planted as to hang directly out over the water." Apparently, Dr. Underhill arrived at this plan after much trial and error to defeat the "curculio," an insect known to destroy plum crops. It "will not sting the fruit that hangs over water."[27]

The abundance of Underhill's vineyards and orchards are clear, as is his thoughtful approach to experimentation and development of a new industry in the Hudson Valley. When he was asked to speak at the American Institute for the Encouragement of Science and Invention on "the grape question," his enthusiasm for the subject was unbridled:

> *The tendrils of the grape have enwrapped the heart of man in every country where it grows. The grape is so delicious, so salutary—diluting the blood, and causing it to flow easily through the veins—and there is nothing equal to it for old age. In this country, its use will grow, will increase until its consumption will be prodigious. It will supplant some of the articles which destroy men, and establish the cheerful body in place of the bloated, diseased systems of the intemperate. No disease of the liver, no dyspepsia are found among those who freely eat the grape.*[28]

In 1851, the American Institute awarded Underhill with a medal for excellence in grape growing.

In addition, Underhill expanded the Newtown Pippin apple orchards of his father and reportedly built eight greenhouses for the production of roses—so, along with his wine grapes, which were sweet enough to sell as fruit, he had a flourishing business selling apples, quince, pears, plums and flowers to New York City and beyond. In fact, crates of Croton Point apples were supposedly sent to Queen Victoria for her wedding breakfast in 1840.

In 1847, Richard Underhill had an elaborate Italianate villa built on the tip of Teller's Point. Using marble quarried by prison labor from nearby Sing Sing, he named it Interwasser, meaning "between the waters"—a nod to its location between the Croton and Haverstraw Bays. One can only imagine the unparalleled views of Hudson River sunsets he must have enjoyed from this idyllic site.

Above: Underhill vineyards scene, *Harper's Weekly*, October 26, 1867. *Image published with permission of ProQuest LLC. Further reproduction is prohibited without permission.*

Right: Medal awarded to Richard T. Underhill in 1851 by the American Institute. *Westchester County Historical Society.*

Opposite, top: Richard T. Underhill's mansion, Interwasser. *Croton Historical Society.*

Opposite, bottom: Site of Richard T. Underhill's Interwasser, circa 2022. *Photo by Scott Craven.*

To protect the view of his new mansion, he successfully fought the Congress of the United States and stopped the construction of a proposed lighthouse on Teller's Point; it was eventually built to the south, near today's Sleepy Hollow. Interwasser would be demolished in 1940, and today all that is left to whisper of this elegant mansion are four large yew trees planted by Dr. Underhill himself and some blocks of marble that lie in front of the modern-day Nature Center to the north.

By 1852, Underhill was selling his grapevines and loaning his vinedressers to help establish small vineyards in New York, Baltimore and Philadelphia, with ambitions to expand as far south as New Orleans.

Underhill's wine became known throughout New York State and received much positive press. Dr. Willard Parker, commissioner of the Metropolitan Board of Health, raved:

> *I have examined the wines from the vineyard of Dr. Underhill and I am confident they are pure and can be relied on as a tonic in sickness and for table use. At this time when wine and spirits are so generally vile compounds whose use is destructive to health, Dr. Underhill confers an incalculably great favor upon the public.*[29]

Other mentions of Underhill's wines include a Christmas Day 1864 review from the *New York Times* affirming that "Dr. Underhill's wines…are made from grapes gathered in the famous Croton Point Vineyards, and their peculiar excellence consists in the fact that they are all pure, and neither drugged, liquored, or watered. They are decidedly the best and safest beverage that ladies can offer to their callers on New Year's Day."[30]

The *New York Herald* enthused that "Dr. Underhill's exquisite native Port Wine is about the best we have ever tasted…this pure article, after being kept in the cellar for a short time, will be equal to any wine that is imported from the London docks."[31]

Richard T.'s nephew, Stephen Underhill (son of brother William), was born on the point in 1837. By the 1860s, he was working with his Uncle Richard and experimenting with grapes. In fact, it is Stephen who is credited with originating the Croton and Senasqua varietals, heirloom grapes that are still grown today.

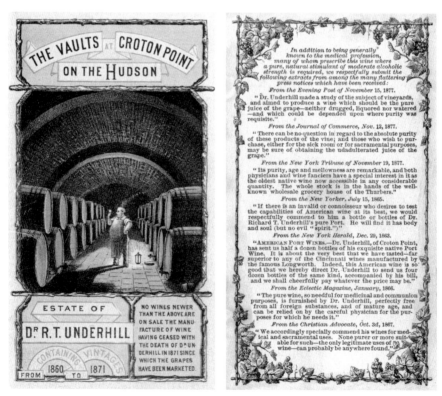

Sales pamphlet for Underhill Vineyard Wines, circa 1871. *Westchester County Historical Society.*

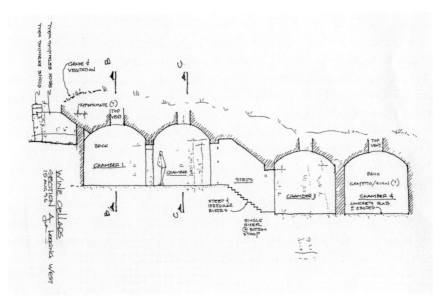

Sketch of Underhill wine cellars, 1996. *Westchester County Archives.*

Both Richard and Stephen were described in U.P. Hedrick's 1904 compendium, *The Grapes of New York*, as "pioneer vineyardists in this state and men of great enterprise and initiative contributing much to American viticulture by precept and example."[32]

Underhill's vineyards were so prolific that he constructed a series of four brick-lined wine cellars in the hill facing Croton Bay to age his bottles and barrels of wine, vinegar and cider. These still stand today, and over the years plans have been made to renovate them and plant an interpretative vineyard nearby. However, the cellars are currently closed to the public and in desperate need of restoration.

By the 1860s, Underhill had engaged the services of Philip Samstag, a German winemaker, to oversee the vineyards.

Dr. Underhill died a bachelor in 1871, and winemaking ceased on Croton Point. His will gives us a glimpse into the varied enterprises he engaged in, as well as the general success of most. He left nearly 30,000 gallons of wine in barrels, 2,080 gallons of vinegar and 160 gallons of cider in his wine vaults, along with numerous bottles of wine. Various boats are listed, along with pigs, cows and horses and miscellaneous items of farm machinery. And Philip Samstag continued living on Croton Point, supervising whatever farming continued until he retired to Ossining. Samstag Avenue in the Crotonville section of the town of Ossining is named after his family.

Underhill wine cellar exterior, 1998. *Photo by Gene Panczenko.*

Underhill wine cellar interior, 1998. *Photo by Gene Panczenko.*

The surviving Underhills couldn't agree on what to do with all the wine stored in the cool vaults on Croton Point, and it took until 1877 for the wine to be brought to market. By the time that happened, it had been aging for several years and was said to have been only improved by the delay.

BRICKMAKING, 1830s–1915[33]

Richard's brother William also grew grapes and tended orchards on his 165 acres of Croton Point at first, but in the 1830s, he also started manufacturing bricks. This would be one of thirty-four brickyards operating in the town of Cortlandt at the time, thanks to the increasing demand for bricks in response to the New York City's Great Fire of 1835, which accelerated the shift from flammable wooden frame buildings to fire-resistant brick ones. The boundless supply of clay deposited during the time of the glacial lakes provided the raw materials for this new market.

At first, William had about sixty-five employees, many living in a large building on the point and doing all the work by hand. As brickmaking became more sophisticated, William partnered with his brother-in-law Richard D. Tallcot, the proprietor of a foundry in Oswego, New York, who designed and manufactured the IXL Special Brick Machine. A narrow-gauge steam train was also constructed around this time.

On Croton Point, the Underhill bricks carried the WAU and IXL logos on them (WAU for "William A. Underhill" and IXL for "I excel"). To this day, you will find hundreds of bricks littering the shore of the point that carry these imprints.

The Underhill brickmaking concern became a family affair. William's sister-in-law Phebe was married to Richard Talcott. William's son Stephen's wife, Elizabeth Wales, took care of the accounting for the business. William's daughter Mary married Richard Walker, who operated the schooners that took the bricks up- and downriver.

There were ultimately two brickyards in operation on the point—maps from 1851 onward indicate that one was located down the hill from the Nature Center, near where the main parking lot is today. The other was located on the flat field just west of the beach area.

The history of brickmaking is one that offers many opportunities to fall down a research hole. People are nuts about bricks: the different styles, the different molds, the frogs, the different logos. Hard brick, pale brick, brown

Top: William A. Underhill "IXL" brick on south beach, Croton Point. *Photo by Scott Craven.*

Middle: William A. Underhill "WAU" brick on south beach, Croton Point. *Photo by Scott Craven.*

Below: Brick drying sheds near Enoch's Point, circa 1910. *Croton Historical Society.*

CLINKER BRICKS

A "clinker" brick is one that was exposed to excessive heat during the firing process, causing it to become deformed or discolored. They get their name from the identifiable *clinking* sound they make when struck. (In the nineteenth century, "ringing" bricks was a common method of determining the quality of a brick.) Though generally discarded by builders who required uniformity, clinkers became popular with the Arts and Crafts movement, as their eccentricities were considered to add visual interest and unique architectural detail. Clinkers also became popular in Colonial Revival-style houses in the early twentieth century because their very irregularities were reminiscent of the pre-industrial era. Today, clinkers are extremely rare due to the automated methods of modern brickmaking.

front, red front—these four are only a very few of the many types of brick fabricated along the Hudson in the nineteenth and early twentieth centuries.

On Croton Point, as elsewhere at the time, brickmaking was a seasonal business. Backbreaking and intricate, the process went something like this: spring through fall, the clay was dug up and placed in a circular pit, where it was mixed with coal dust and sand. The mixture was fed into the IXL brickmaking machine, molded into bricks and then left for a few days in a drying area.

Once solidified enough to handle, the bricks went into a kiln and were fired for about a week. The foundation of one of these kilns, a "scove kiln," was discovered on Croton Point by fluke in 2000 when a tree toppled over and exposed it. It was then partially excavated.

Brickmaking was a complex endeavor and based on the number of deformed bricks ("clinkers") one still finds on the shores of Croton Point, it seems that a fair number of bricks were discarded. Those that were only slightly flawed were given to the laborers to use. In fact, a number of homes in the village of Croton were reportedly built by brickyard workers with these discarded bricks.[34]

Many buildings were built on the point to support this business. According to a 2004 study of Croton Point, "A small community developed around the yards...a school was built for the worker's children [as well as] a store, a tavern,

The fruit house (also used as a boardinghouse.) *Photo by Scott Craven.*

Old school building. *Photo by Scott Craven.*

Brickyard workers, circa 1910. *Carl Oeschner.*

and a boarding house for seasonal workers."[35] Maps and aerial photographs from the twentieth century indicate other buildings and possibly other boardinghouses along the south and west side of Teller's Point.

According to various early twentieth-century censuses, the workers at the Croton Point brickyards were a mixed group. From Black families who came up from the South in an early wave of the Great Migration to immigrants from Italy, Holland, Finland, Sweden and Germany, they all worked side by side—just as in the rest of the county at the time.

There were about two hundred people living on the point during this period—some families, but more single men who were boarding. It's hard to imagine that sort of population density on Croton Point today, even when all the campgrounds are full.

According to the 1890 Annual Report of the State Geologist, the clay on Croton Point was considered "fat," meaning that it possessed "great plasticity and is very pure."[36] The report further noted that the bricks made on Croton Point were "of very good quality, being used for outsides and selling for $14.50 per 1,000."[37]

William Underhill died in 1873, and son Stephen gave up his experimentation with grape varieties to take over the brickyards. William's

FAMILY LIFE ON THE POINT

The Nabors and Dykstra families lived on the point in the early 1900s. Thomas and Minnie Nabors came up from Virginia in 1910 with their three small children, Francell, Edwin and Pearl. They lived on the bottom floor of the fruit house year-round from about 1911 until 1915, with Thomas working as a laborer in the brickyards and Minnie cooking for the boarders. When the brickyards closed, they moved to Ossining and purchased a home on Hunter Street, where Thomas built a successful trucking business delivering coal and oil.*

Dirk and Mary Dykstra emigrated from Holland in the early 1900s. Dirk quickly made his way to Croton Point, where he worked as an engineer on the brickyard's narrow-gauge railway. Mary would have at least eight children in fifteen years, dying in childbirth in 1916 at the age of thirty-eight. Dirk left Croton Point when the brickyards closed, moved to Mount Airy Road in Croton and worked in Ossining for many years as a car mechanic.

---

* Sandra Mann Michael, granddaughter to the Naborses, conversation with the author, February 2022.

Left: Thomas and Minnie Nabors, with Francell, Edwin and Pearl, circa 1911. *Sandra Michael.*

Right: Dirk and Mary Dykstra and family, circa 1914. *Croton Historical Society.*

estate contained many of the same items as his brother's, just fewer of them. Who's to say that the old hay rake that sits quietly in front of the Fruit House today didn't belong to one of the Underhill brothers?

The inventory of the brickyards in William's will is impressive, with more than 3 million bricks in the south brickyard alone and a long list of machines and steam engines. The contents of the Fruit House also give us a glimpse

Hay Rake by the fruit house. *Photo by Scott Craven.*

W.A. Underhill Company steam shovel. *Kirk Moldoff.*

into the agricultural endeavors pursued on the point at the time, with apples, buckwheat, rye, turnips, potatoes and hay stored there.

By 1886, Stephen Underhill had several hundred workers and was able to produce about sixty-four thousand Croton Front bricks per day, in addition to enameled bricks used for tiling and wainscoting.

Today, when you walk along the field south of the main parking lot, if you catch it in just the right light, you can see a low ridge running through the stands of mulberry and willow trees. This is precisely where the narrow-gauge railroad track ran, connecting the clay pits off West Beach with the brick making buildings.

By 1899, the Underhills had sold their interest in the brickyards, which continued operating for about fifteen more years.

OTHER INDUSTRIAL ACTIVITIES ON CROTON POINT

While the Underhills owned the majority of the point, the Van Cortlandt family continued to own much of the Croton Neck area where the railroad tracks first cut through in 1847.

Impossible to see today, the Croton Neck plateau originally extended much farther east, all the way across what is now the extensive Croton-Harmon rail yards and Route 9, meeting up at the same level with South Riverside Avenue in Croton-on-Hudson. Millions of cubic feet of sand left over from the delta of the glacial lake have been excavated to make way for the railroads and highway. Much of this excavated sand was used as fill all over the Hudson Valley and as far south as New York City.

In 1874, the *New York Times* detailed such a sale: "Mr. Pierre Van Cortlandt has sold 400,000 cubic yards of sand…to be used for the purpose of filling in the cattle yards of the Hudson River Railroad Company at Fifty-ninth Street. One hundred Italians have reached Croton Landing to take up the sand."[38] Who knows what artifacts might have been transported away from Croton Point over the years to sit quietly on the shores of the Hudson in Manhattan today?

As the brickyards began to wind down at the beginning of the twentieth century, investors, industrialists and the government competed to find new uses for this unique piece of land. Some of the ideas will surprise you.

GRAPES AND BRICKS CHRONOLOGY

1690s

According to legend, Captain William Kidd (1655–1701) buries his pirate gold on Croton Point.

1804

Robert Underhill purchases land on Croton Point.

1829

Robert Underhill dies. Sons Richard T. and William take over their father's Croton Point land. Richard establishes the first award-winning vineyard in the Northeast.

1830s

William Underhill starts manufacturing bricks on the north side of the point.

1847

Interwasser, an Italianate villa, is built by Dr. Richard T. Underhill on Teller's Point.

Portion of Croton Neck is cut through for railroad tracks.

1871

Dr. Richard T. Underhill dies.

1873

William Underhill dies, and winemaking stops; son Stephen takes over the family brickyards.

1895

Underhill brickyards are mortgaged and then sold.

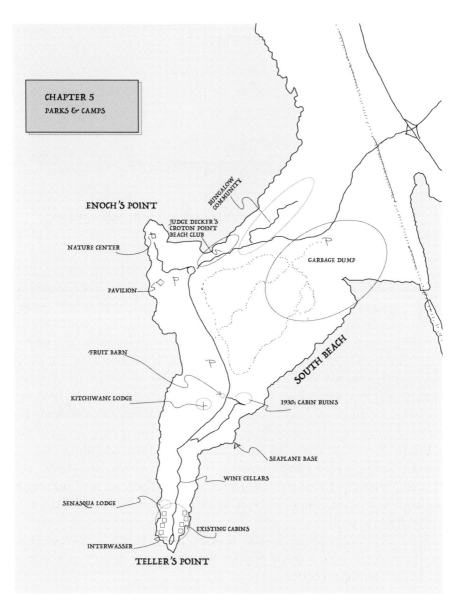

ENOCH'S POINT

BUNGALOW COMMUNITY

JUDGE DECKER'S CROTON POINT BEACH CLUB

NATURE CENTER

GARBAGE DUMP

PAVILION

FRUIT BARN

SOUTH BEACH

KITCHIWANC LODGE

1930s CABIN RUINS

SEAPLANE BASE

WINE CELLARS

SENASQUA LODGE

EXISTING CABINS

INTERWASSER

TELLER'S POINT

Sketch map of parks and camps. *Map by Harrison Isaac.*

Chapter 5

PARKS AND CAMPS

It is by common consent, a good thing for people to get back to nature.
—Aldo Leopold

T hroughout the nineteenth century, Croton Point was privately owned, primarily by the Underhill and Van Cortlandt families, and its uses were agricultural and industrial.

Starting around 1900, even though the brickyards were still quite active, the point's proximity to the city and its unique combination of land and river access made it a popular site for camping and leisure activities. As various parcels on the point were mortgaged and sold off, other land use ideas for the point evolved. These unrealized plans included building an enormous shipyard for government use, a transatlantic shipping terminal, a bridge that would span the Hudson between Croton and Rockland, an aircraft factory, a Ford Motor factory, a veterans rehabilitation hospital, the United Nations (yes, really), a county airport, a heliport for mail delivery, a garbage incinerator, a marina for pleasure craft, a golf course, restaurants and a dirt bike trail.

None of these projects came to fruition. By 1923, the point had been purchased by Westchester County for the creation of a park as well as a dump for municipal refuse.

PARKS ON CROTON POINT

In the early 1900s, Judge Frank Decker, then the Croton justice of the peace, leased the beach fronting Haverstraw Bay and founded the Croton Point Beach Club. He built a primitive bathhouse, clubhouse and simple beach bungalows. The "genial Judge" was called "the well-known, smiling apotheosis of Father Neptune who keeps vigilant guard on the health and morals of Croton Point."[39]

His connection to Croton Point was deep. He, his father and several family members had lived on and worked in the brickyards on Croton Point, at least as far back as the 1880s. It must have given Judge Decker more than a little satisfaction to enjoy the point for leisure purposes in his later years.

At first, Judge Decker's bungalow colony consisted of platform tents built directly on the beach, just steps away from Haverstraw Bay. Then, simple wooden bungalows replaced the tents on the beach. Eventually, the colony would cover the beach and extend up to the plateau.

Judge Decker's bungalow colony was near the brickyards, which continued operating for more than a decade. What must it have been like to stand on the beach then, with the small-gauge trains carting clay to the kilns and the finished bricks to the piers, the steam ships regularly docking to pick up pallets of bricks to take to the city and the bells alerting the workers to shift changes? The twice-daily explosions across the river at the gravel quarries would have added to the industrial cacophony along the mighty river.

The brickyards on Croton Point ceased operation in about 1915, the clay pits finally exhausted from more than eighty years of excavations. By then, the recreational potential of the point was clear. In 1912, Point

Frank Decker - Mrs Decker about 1908

Opposite: Judge and Mrs. Frank Decker. *Croton Historical Society*.

This page, top: Croton Point Beach Club circa 1909 *Croton Historical Society*.

This page, bottom: Croton Point Clubhouse on the Hudson, 1908. *Croton Historical Society*.

Point Pleasant Park postcard, 1914. *Croton Historical Society.*

Pleasant Park had opened on Teller's Point. Using Richard T. Underhill's Interwasser mansion as its main draw, it offered picnicking on the lawn and bathing on the rocky south shore beach, along with music, dancing, boating and fishing.

According to early environmentalist Theodore Cornu, steamers brought day trippers up from New York City, docking at a southern pier off Teller's Point—likely the same pier used back in Underhill's day for shipping his fruit, roses and wine to the city. Various groups also camped on the point, the American Canoe Club being one of the earliest and most well dressed, it seems.

Other exciting diversions that could be found on Croton Point at the time were private seaplane rides, arranged by Judge Decker and the Croton Point Aero Club. Consisting of a three-seater Curtiss MF Flying Boat, interested parties could take short flights up and down the Hudson at the princely cost of fifteen dollars per person.

The seaplanes had come to Croton Point as early as 1918, when popular Broadway figures (and local residents) Margaret Mayo, Edgar Selwyn and Holbrook Blinn, along with their neighbor, author/humorist Irvin S. Cobb, purchased 350-acres of land on the point, incorporating themselves as the Croton Point Company with an eye toward developing a small "aero club." Air flight was a new and intriguing technology, one that was evolving rapidly

Left: Point Pleasant Park postcard, steamer docking on south pier, circa 1914. *Croton Historical Society.*

Below: Campers, American Canoe Club, 1916. *Croton Historical Society.*

thanks to World War I.

According to the *Rockland County Times*, the plan of the Croton Point Company was to train "aviators and for the development of the science of aeronautical and kindred sciences, creation of public sentiment and support for the aeronautical protection of the Hudson Valley."[40]

But their $100 shares stayed firmly in their stock certificate book, and by 1921, they had sold their interest to "a number of former aces in the aviation service of the Foreign Legion." These aces reportedly planned to

Curtiss MF Flying Boat, circa 1918. *Croton Historical Society.*

build "mammoth plane hangars which will house superhydroaeroplanes intended for transcontinental passenger service."[41]

Nothing seemed to have come of this aero enterprise either, but by 1929, Westchester County was seriously considering building a county airport on Croton Point. Perhaps the stock market crash made the county rethink its priorities because this plan went nowhere.

However, in 1931, J. Noel Macy, a publisher of a chain of Westchester County newspapers and the son of V. Everitt Macy, a former Westchester County parks commissioner, established a private seaplane base of his own on the south beach of Croton Point.

Noel Macy had been behind the earlier plan to build a county airport on Croton Point. When the county lost interest, Macy took the lead. Leasing land on Croton Point from the parks commission for $100 per year, Macy spent about $10,000 to build a small hangar on the south beach that could house two amphibian-type planes, as well as a separate structure housing a small electric power plant.

In 1935, plans were again afoot to build a county airport on Croton Point, this time using $2.5 million of Works Progress Administration (WPA) money. While this did not happen, at least not to the tune of millions of dollars, a 214-foot emergency landing strip was constructed in 1936 where today's RV park is located. In 1941, another emergency landing field was constructed, this time for possible wartime use, in the area where the parking lots are located today. Both were only used a few times by planes experiencing engine problems.

THE COUNTY TAKES OVER THE POINT

In 1923, Robert William Justice, founder and director of the New York Academy of Business, established the Croton Development Corporation, consisting of a group of Harlem businessmen who hoped to develop an elaborate country club on Croton Point, with "playgrounds, churches, and a bathing beach but a few of the features…there will also be facilities for outings and excursions, a large baseball park and athletic oval, with the finest facilities for every recreational activity."[42]

Justice had a handshake deal to purchase about three hundred acres of Croton Point from Inglis Uppercu, of the Detroit Cadillac Corporation, for $425,000. However, at the last minute, possibly due to strident complaints from locals, Westchester County purchased the land for a mere $360,000—significantly less than the Croton Development Corporation would have paid.

At the time of these negotiations, the *Croton-Harmon News* reprinted an article from the *Peekskill Evening Star* entitled "Will Colored People Have Croton Point?" and noted that "[a]nxiety is reported to be spreading in the neighborhood of Croton Point, for property-owners there fear that instead of this development increasing the value of the land there, there will be an immediate depreciation."[43]

On August 28, 1923, the *New York Times* reported that "the Westchester

Inglis Uppercu (1877–1944) was the owner of the very profitable Detroit Cadillac Corporation, an early car dealership in the New York–New Jersey area. He was also an early aeroplane enthusiast, involved in the creation of Aeromarine Airways, which got its start flying seaplane sightseeing jaunts in New York Harbor and up the Hudson River. Thanks to Prohibition (1920–33), Aeromarine was one of the first airlines to fly regularly scheduled flights, becoming extremely popular with the wealthy, who would fly from Key West, Florida, to Cuba and the Caribbean in order to drink legally. It seems likely that when Uppercu purchased land on Croton Point, he was eyeing it for development as a potential airbase.

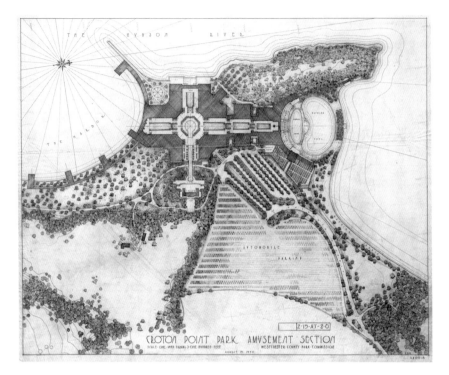

Croton Point Park Amusement Section, blueprint, circa 1924. *Westchester County Archives.*

County Park Commission stepped in yesterday and bought Croton Point…a few hours after a syndicate of Harlem negroes announced it expected to purchase a 300-acre tract for an all-year negro 'Atlantic City.'"[44] Justice was quoted as saying:

> *It is a great surprise and blow to me. The fact is that anti-negro sentiment, especially in Peekskill which is a hotbed of racial feeling, forced the sale to the county. We had an oral option…for the land to make it into a park for the best element of colored people and it was the best element of our race from all over the country we expected to bring there.*[45]

In addition to purchasing Inglis Uppercu's parcel, Westchester County acquired other acreage, planning to build a lavish park. Uppercu, operating with several partners as the East Hudson Development Company, had purchased Judge Decker's bungalow colony in 1921, expanding it to add a tent colony on the plateau and a dance hall, turning it into what was called the "Playground of Westchester" by the *White Plains Reporter*.[46]

Upon the sale to the county, though, the beach area was cleared of all structures, graded and opened to the public. The county tried to evict the tent colony altogether, but the outrage was so great that it compromised, even agreeing to install plumbing and electricity to service the colony. Soon after, next to the beach, on the Mother's Lap portion of the park where one of the brickyards had been located, an amusement park was developed. Called the Hudson River Development Company and operated by the Paulson family, it contained shooting galleries, merry-go-rounds, a Ferris wheel and bumper cars.

The county-run Croton Point Park officially opened on June 6, 1924, with just a primitive bathhouse on the beach. About 250,000 people were said to have visited the park that first year.

SUMMER CAMPS

Summer camps were established on Teller's Point—Camp Kitchawanc for boys and Camp Senasqua for girls. In 1925, the cost for a camper was $6.50 per week, and an article in the *Scarsdale Inquirer* trumpeted the fact that "Two Hundred Children Gain Ton of Weight at Croton Camp." The fact that this rated a headline gives insight to the living conditions of city children at the time, even in that Roaring Twenties/pre-Depression era. The article goes on to highlight one girl "who gained seventeen pounds in one week, a direct result of the out-of-door life."[47]

Vestiges of these camps still stand in the form of the Senasqua and Kitchawanc Lodges. And at least one cabin from that old summer camp era sits quietly amid the more recently built cabins on Teller's Point. Today, if you walk down the road from the RV camp toward Croton Bay, past the brick groundskeeper's house, you might be even able to see the ruins of one of the old Camp Kitchawanc cabins on your left, almost down at the shore.

Another interesting recreational use for Croton Point was the progressive Mothers' Rest Camp, organized in 1928, headquartered at Interwasser. Separate camp programs for children ages three through nine were arranged so that mothers could get their rest. At its high point, more than eight hundred children and two hundred mothers, in two-week sessions, were enjoying the sunshine and fresh air of the Hudson Valley.

At the risk of idealizing the past, it does seem like the Croton Point camps would have been special places. In the 1960s, on the occasion of the camps' closing (and absorption by the Mountain Lakes Camp in South Salem, New

Boy campers in front of tent, circa 1930s. *Croton Historical Society.*

Campers saluting the flag, circa 1930s. *Westchester County Archives.*

WESTCHESTER COUNTY SUMMER CAMPS
FOR BOYS AND GIRLS • JUNE 28—AUGUST 23, 1937

At Croton Point

For the 11th consecutive season, the Westchester County Recreation Commission will conduct summer camps at Croton Point for boys between the ages of 8 and 16 and for girls from 8 to 14 years of age. Registrations should be made at once. Camp Kitchawanc in the middle of the Point at Indian Shell Mounds accommodates 160 boys at one time, while Senasqua, the girls' camp on the far end of the Point holds 130 campers. Only children living in Westchester County may attend these and the outpost units, Camp Brownell and Camp Fahnestock.

VARIED PROGRAM

Opening on June 28 and continuing to August 23, the camp program will include outdoor activities of all kinds, nature study, games, overnight hiking expeditions and swimming. Delightful hours are spent in the crafts shops and nature museum, while under the trees, children may join in music,

At Camp Brownell

The thrill of the old West, the lore of the cow-puncher and plainsman, will live again at Camp Brownell for the limited group of campers who choose this outpost unit. Under the same general supervision and with a leader who was himself once a cowboy — G. Wade Ferguson — Brownell boys will lead a more primitive outdoor life than that at Croton Point.

Emphasis will be place on cultivating a deep-seated love of the 'great open spaces,' and an understanding of animal, bird and plant life. Camp Brownell is surrounded by 300 acres of wild woodland and hills, divided by deep flowing streams.

The activities will be coordinated in a Western program in which not only sports such as lassooing will have a part, but also the music and traditional background of pioneer days in the West.

Young campers suited by taste and aptitude for the rough out-of-door life will want to join this group, and registrations should be made now.

dancing and impromptu dramatics. With many campers, art or pottery are favorite hobbies, while some prefer the hardier sports or the fascinating study of Indian lore on this site which once was a camping ground for Indian tribes.

REFRESHING AND HEALTHFUL EXPERIENCE

The children are invited to spend vacations ranging from two to eight weeks at camp. During these holiday periods, the health of every child at the Croton Camps is held of paramount importance and activities leading to over-stimulation are discouraged. Camp Administrator Cranford considers it the camp's first responsibility to send campers—as well as councilors—back to their homes refreshed and rested. In carrying out this policy, the camp has the cooperation of Grasslands Hospital and an individual guidance service conducted with the assistance of the Westchester County Children's Association.

PROGRESSIVE PLAN

The Westchester camps are planned according to the highest standards of progressive camping. Charles B. Cranford, Administrator, is a former instructor in the School of Education at New York University, and he has gathered together college-trained councilors whose understanding of educational methods and recreation leadership is unquestioned.

Campers are encouraged to choose their own forms of play and work, tending to develop native talents, initiative and self-reliance, but always under the friendly guidance of experienced leaders.

GOOD APPETITES FOR GOOD FOOD

Brisk appetites are well-satisfied at camp where a dietitian of recognized standing supervises the menu of good food, prepared by experienced cooks, is a factor in the health building program for every child. Meals are well-balanced and varied.

UNUSUALLY LOW FEE

The fee, exclusive of transportation to and from camp, is $8.50 per week, unusually low because the camps are non-profit making and county-operated. The camps may be reached by automobile via the Albany Post Road through Terrytown and Ossining to Harmon-on-Hudson, N. Y., and by train to Harmon Station, 2 miles from camp.

EQUIPMENT

Campers are reminded to bring a bathing suit, rubbers and raincoat, durable play clothing, night gown or pajamas, 3 sheets, an extra blanket, small pillow and slip, a tin cup, soap, comb, brush and tooth brush, a sweater or coat, a play suit, 2 pairs of shoes, musical instruments, and additional clothing if laundry is to be sent out.

At Fahnestock Park

Branching out last summer to take care of the increase in campers at Croton Point, the Westchester camps opened a new outpost camp in Clarence Fahnestock Park in cooperation with the Taconic State Park Commission. In this beautiful 3400-acre reservation, a base unit is established on 5 acres of clearing. The boys who make the trek to this frontier camp live in lean-to's, tepees and tents, eating meals cooked over open fires.

The same type of guidance and all health regulation, followed at Croton Point are the rule here, but the program is planned to suit the 'close-to-nature' atmosphere. Robert Walter O'Kane, veteran pioneer camper, will be in charge under the direction of Mr. Cranford.

A 1937 brochure for Westchester County Camps. *Westchester County Historical Society.*

York), Sal J. Prezioso, then the commissioner of the Westchester Parks and Recreation Department, wrote that at Croton Point "discovery of historical legendry has excited campers: from Indian arrowheads to the ruins of old wine cellars and remnants of an old Brick Factory."[48]

Various other camps would take over this site—a music camp, a "handicapped camp" and RV, cabin and tent family camps. As of 2022, these last three are still available for public use.

THE CLEARWATER FESTIVAL

One of the most popular and long-lived gatherings on the point in recent memory is the Great Hudson River Revival. Originally founded by Pete Seeger in the mid-1960s as an itinerant folk festival raising funds to build the *Clearwater*, an iconic sloop that would come to symbolize environmental advocacy, the Revival came to Croton Point in 1978. Using music, dance and storytelling, it would attract thousands and become the country's largest environmental celebration. Although pollution from the landfill forced it to relocate briefly, by the late 1990s the Revival, renamed the Clearwater Festival, had returned, continuing its mission of environmental education and consciousness-raising through the arts.

GARBAGE DUMP NO MORE

Throughout the development of these various camps and parks, the dump in the middle grew and grew, polluting Croton Point and the Hudson River.

After a protracted fight, the landfill was closed for good in 1986. As the capping process began, the county began to plan an expansive redevelopment of the point, which included a marina, a wave pool, a restaurant, a nine-hole golf course, tennis courts and an off-road motorbike trail. While most of these more ambitious projects were shelved, the county did upgrade and expand the camping areas, as well as redevelop the parking, picnic and playground spaces around Enoch's Point.

When the capping of the landfill was completed in 1993, native plants were carefully chosen to cover the former eyesore and attract local birds and pollinators. Today, it all just looks like a natural feature of the landscape. Soon after, football and baseball fields were installed at the entrance to the park, and a Nature Center was established on Enoch's Point. Today, there is a model airplane field on the plateau; popular RV, tent and cabin camping sites; and various annual festivals on the point. A new bathhouse is in the process of being built.

Croton Point continues to evolve.

———<◈>———

PARKS AND CAMPS CHRONOLOGY
1900s
Judge Decker's Bungalow Colony—the Croton Point Beach Club—is established on the north beach, where today's swimming area is located.

1912
Point Pleasant Park is established on Teller's Point.

1923

Robert William Justice of the Croton Point Development Company tries to buy land to develop what the *New York Times* calls a "Negro Atlantic City."[49]

Westchester County purchases 350 acres plus an additional 150 acres of Croton Point for development into a County Park; 70 acres are set aside to be used as a local garbage dump.

1924

"New" Croton Point Park opens to the public, under the auspices of Westchester County (June 6).

1925

Summer Camps Kitchawanc and Senasqua are established by the Westchester County Recreation Commission and opened to local boys and girls.

1928

Mothers' Rest Camp is established in Underhill Mansion on Teller's Point.

1930

WPA project plants fifteen-acre forest of white pine, Scotch pine and Norway spruce on south slope of point, some of which are still standing today.

1931

J. Noel Macy establishes a private seaplane base on the south side of Croton Point.

1940

The Interwasser mansion demolished.

1986

The landfill closes.

1991

The landfill capping project completed.

———◇———

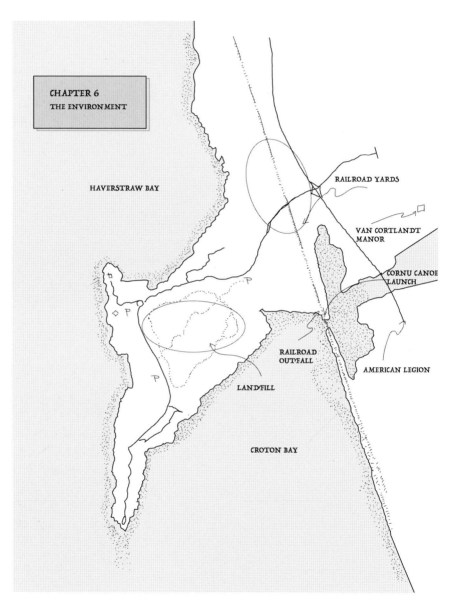

CHAPTER 6
THE ENVIRONMENT

HAVERSTRAW BAY

RAILROAD YARDS

VAN CORTLANDT
MANOR

CORNU CANOE
LAUNCH

RAILROAD
OUTFALL

AMERICAN LEGION

LANDFILL

CROTON BAY

Sketch map of environmental history. *Map by Harrison Isaac.*

Chapter 6

ENVIRONMENTAL MOVEMENTS

Never doubt that a small group of thoughtful, committed citizens can change the world. Indeed, it's the only thing that ever has.
—Margaret Meade

Croton Point is a big part of the reason the Hudson River is so much cleaner today. By the twentieth century, the pollution from industry and railroads had destroyed the river. The water smelled, the fish were dangerous to eat and Con Edison was trying lop the top off Storm King Mountain to the north to create a pumped storage hydroelectric facility.

On Croton Point, such contamination was even more concentrated, as it combined that of the river with the municipal waste that had been dumped in its wetlands since the late 1920s. In addition, since 1847, the railroad had been continuously enlarging a valley through the old delta to allow passage of the east shore rail and its ever-expanding work yards. These railyards habitually dumped waste oil into the river, often enveloping the point and the lower Croton River with a choking slick.

It wasn't until the 1960s that the environmental movement came to Croton Point. In response to the increasing desecration of America's historic river and spurred on by the landmark environmental lawsuit that eventually prevented Con Edison from destroying Storm King Mountain, two separate styles of

NEW YORK CENTRAL RAILROAD

The rail yards at Croton are a massive, looming presence on Croton Point—so much so that many do not think the point even starts until after you have crossed the tracks. In fact, the yards are actually located about halfway out onto the delta portion of the point. In 1847, when hundreds of thousands of cubic yards of sand were excavated from Croton Neck for the first rail line, the point was still relatively intact. But that would soon change.

A 1902 train crash caused authorities to prohibit steam trains from entering the island of Manhattan, and the railroad quickly needed to find a convenient place to switch from steam to electric locomotives. Croton Point's marshland and easily quarried sand ridge offered the perfect solution.

environmentalism were born on the point. Creating a complementary force, these two styles would prove unstoppable.

What were the secrets to their success? Proximity to New York City and institutions of higher learning, as well as the historical significance of the river, certainly played a part. But it was the variety of concerned people, uniting across economic, educational and political lines, that really made the difference.

THE FIGHTERS

One type of environmentalism was antagonistic and in your face. Characterized by zealous lawyers and writers who weren't afraid to wear waders and handle fish, they teamed up with working folks who had spent their lives fishing on and appreciating the river. Utilizing old laws and new science, they confronted the polluters and refused to back down.

An important catalyst for this movement was Robert Boyle, a writer for *Sports Illustrated*, a fisherman, a former Marine Corps officer and a popular "CPD" (Croton Point Denizen). He commuted from Croton to the city and often went fishing right after he walked off the train. Boyle wrote the seminal work *The Hudson River, a Natural and Unnatural History*, devoting entire chapters to Haverstraw Bay and the Croton River.

On March 18, 1966, in the Parker-Bale American Legion Hall in Crotonville, Robert Boyle addressed a mixed group of grave diggers, dentists, construction workers and commercial fisherman, rallying them to fight the polluters. Prodding folks who would have been much happier pulling up crab traps than speaking to lawyers, he helped form them into the Hudson River Fisherman's Association (HRFA), a powerful grass-roots organization. Ultimately, the group would testify in front of Congress, take on Con Edison and General Electric and help spark a worldwide environmental movement. But its initial sights were set on something much closer to home: Croton Point.

The initial target of the newly formed HRFA was the Penn Central Railroad's waste pipe at the junction of Croton Point and the Croton River. With the incoming tide pushing the sheen of oil up the Croton River and the outgoing tide spreading it across the southern beaches of the point, this creator of oil slicks was an equal-opportunity polluter. One of Robert Boyle's greatest

Crotonville

In the shadow of Croton Point, General Electric's Global Learning Crotonville Leadership John F. Welch Center trains future leaders for GE's multinational corporation. GE has been in a long-standing fight over the cleanup of the polychlorinated biphenyls (PCBs) that it has dumped into the Hudson. The irony is profound—the birthplace of the HRFA just down the hill from the bunker-like security entrance to the GE Crotonville campus. Poetically, a 75mm pack howitzer sits in front of the American Legion Hall today, pointing up the hill like an accusing finger.

American Legion Post Parker Bale Post No. 1597. *Photo by Scott Craven.*

Riverkeeper

The premier advocate for protecting the Hudson River today, the Riverkeeper organization was created in the shadow of Croton Point. From organizing cleanups to litigation to patrolling the Hudson, it advocates for clean water on many fronts. Today, its office is located on the Ossining waterfront. *Riverkeeper.org.*

---

contributions to the fight had been unearthing the Refuse Act of 1899, an old federal law that allowed watchdogs to receive part of the fines imposed on polluters. When the HRFA won its fight with Penn Central, it received $2,000—its portion of the fine collected by the government. The fine from these violations was the fuel that initially allowed the group to push forward.

Soon after, the HRFA joined Scenic Hudson in the landmark fight against Con Ed's Storm King pump storage facility, forever changing the landscape of environmental law and establishing environmentalism as a science.

In 1986, the Hudson River Fisherman's Association changed its name to Riverkeeper. This progressive organization continues to take the lead on almost every single environmental issue in the Hudson Valley. Deploying a thirty-one-foot wooden patrol boat, the *R. Ian Fletcher*, it monitors water quality and looks for polluters along the entire length of the tidal portion of the river and beyond.

The Educators

The other type of environmentalists in this determined and effective movement were the advocates who felt that education was the way forward: the more people learned about the river and what a special place it was, the more they would want to save it.

By the twentieth century, far too many residents of the valley knew little to nothing about the river, having been walled off from it by railroad tracks, industry and pollution. Just a century earlier, the river had been the center of social and commercial interests: boat and canoe clubs, skating, even driving on the frozen river were commonplace, and the river was the key transportation artery for the raw materials that were being used to build the great city to the south.

These educators used the river itself as their classroom, through traditional boats, music and storytelling. Combining their efforts with environmental science, they taught the residents of the valley about the river—its history, its importance and its peril.

The spiritual leader of this grass-roots push to help people understand the river was Theodore Cornu. Cornu discovered the Croton River and its point in the waning days of the nineteenth-century canoe craze. Originally from New York City, he would venture up the Hudson in a touring canoe and camp on the Croton River. Cornu would eventually live in the Van Cortlandt Ferry

Theodore Cornu, 1975. *Croton Historical Society.*

House on that same river. He would commute into Manhattan, where he worked as a calligrapher and illustrator of certificates. He spent the next few decades exploring the valley in a series of small boats and canoes he made by hand and stored in the rafters of the Ferry House. Then as now, these small paddling craft are well suited to exploring the littoral Hudson, with a draft so shallow they can slip under the railroad tracks and float in the shallowest water.

Theodore Cornu would ultimately create the Hudson Valley Echoes, a loose organization of like-minded citizens who wanted to save the river. His hand-drawn newsletters and membership certificates were exquisitely illustrated, with text often written in wavy lines as an homage to the river. These newsletters would contain America's Conservation Pledge in the banner and would end with a plea for help: "Enroll as an 'Echo with the Hudson Valley Echoes, a league of conservation-minded people, willing to cooperate by contributing their talents and skills in the preservation and use of the Hudson River for river purpose. *No dues, no assessments.*" Works of art, these old newsletters and Echo certificates are talismans of the early environmental movement.

Cornu's artistic and educational vision are carried on to this day in the form of the *Clearwater*, a 106-foot, single-masted replica of an old Hudson River sloop. In the 1960s, renowned folk singer and river activist Pete Seeger read a book about the old sailing vessels of the river. This inspired him and others to raise the money to commission a replica of one of these sloops to be built in Maine and brought to the valley.

Above: Hudson Valley Echoes certificate. *Photo by Scott Craven.*

Left: The sloop *Clearwater*, the iconic environmental vessel. *Photo by Scott Craven.*

> At the turn of the twentieth century, canoes (and bicycles) were seen as the future of travel in that pre–mass transit, pre-automobile time. Often decked and propelled with a double-bladed paddle, these canoes could also be fitted with masts and sails. The American Canoe Association frequently held "regattas" on Croton Point.

Traveling up and down the Hudson River with the message of environmental stewardship, the *Clearwater* was originally met with some resistance. Called the "Commie Cutter,"[50] unwelcomed and challenged by some locals, it is now a beloved fixture on the river. A waterborne platform for river education and symbol of the environmental movement, it still provides public sails as well as field trips for local schoolchildren.

THE LANDFILL

In 1923, when Westchester County found itself in possession of Croton Point, most of the middle portion of the point was tidal wetland. At that time, wetlands were considered breeding grounds for disease and were filled in whenever possible. So, two of the first things the county did was to establish a municipal dump in the northeast corner of the swamp and fill in another portion of the swamp to create a new park road.

As the county grew, so did the stream of municipal waste ending up on Croton Point. It was impossible to grow up in the area in the 1960s and 1970s and not be aware of "The Dump." Rumors about what, or who, was buried there abounded. We know for certain that there was a radium-contaminated house buried there, as well as at least one horse euthanized by a vet. Poor early recordkeeping prevents us from ever knowing the full extent of what's in that pile.

Huge tractor trailers filled with garbage were an everyday sight on Route 9, and the ever-present cloud of gulls over the point never let anyone forget exactly what was out there. (A local rugby club that played games on the point had flying gulls on their uniform's crest.)

With the Village of Croton taking on the burden for most of the county's garbage, by the 1950s residents had begun calling for the closing of the dump. Fires, constant heavy truck traffic and the ever-present specter of

Truck loaded with municipal waste being weighed at entrance to Croton Point, 1986. *Westchester County Archives.*

unseen toxins sat like a pall over this small community. Watching the dump burn from the Ossining waterfront became a common occurrence, and in 1986, the chief investigator for Riverkeeper referred to the mound of garbage as "the single worst manmade atrocity on the Hudson."[51]

Sometime in the 1960s, the point became a sanitary landfill, a municipal dump where layers of dirt were spread and compacted over the layers of garbage on a regular basis to mitigate odors and flying debris. While this was a step forward in managing the waste piling up on the point, it allowed even more waste to be deposited. Daily, enormous bulldozers would spread the garbage over the ever-growing mound after tractor trailers had dumped their loads.

Despite its new status as a sanitary landfill, local environmental groups began filing lawsuits to shut it down. The county was rapidly being placed in the untenable position of being forced to close the landfill with no viable options for managing this endless garbage stream. A federal lawsuit brought by the Hudson River Fisherman's Association in 1972 was the beginning of the end—the judge described the landfill as an "environmental time

> ## MUNICIPAL SOLID WASTE
>
> According to the U.S. Environmental Protection Agency, in 1960 Americans produced on average 2.68 pounds of municipal waste per day. By 2018, it had almost doubled to 4.9 pounds per day. Lest anyone think we're not aware of our own culpability in this mess, some quick math leads us to believe that by the time we had graduated high school, we had each contributed thirteen tons of garbage to the point's landfill ourselves.

bomb." By 1975, Westchester County was forced to sign an agreement to close it, although it would linger for more than a decade, instead of the promised six months.

Ideas for what to do with the county's garbage were varied, and in retrospect, many seem absurd. One scheme was to barge the garbage across the river and start filling in the open pit gravel quarry just south of Haverstraw. In response, Rockland residents immediately proposed barging their garbage over to Westchester. Another proposal was to build incinerators on Croton Point and down the river, dumping the residual ash in the Hudson River as fill for the proposed superhighway that would stretch along the shoreline from the Tappan Zee Bridge to Beacon.

With the advent of new technology that allowed municipal waste to be incinerated and converted into electricity, the county was finally able to close the landfill in 1986; by the time the landfill was capped, enough garbage had been deposited there to fill the Empire State Building seven and a half times.

Today, almost all of Westchester County's municipal waste goes to Peekskill, where it is incinerated and turned it into electricity. (90 percent of this waste is dispersed by high-intensity combustion, and the remaining 10 percent is currently being trucked to an ash landfill in eastern Connecticut.) Ironically, today, standing on the old landfill and looking north, you can clearly see the plume of steam being created by this waste-to-energy plant. But this technology is also quickly aging, and people are searching for better, even more environmentally friendly options.

In 1990, the county began the complex process of capping the landfill. Closing Croton Point Park for almost three years and spending more than $24 million, the process began with up to one hundred trucks per day bringing clean fill to cover the garbage pile. That took months to accomplish.

This page, top: Bulldozer on dump. *Westchester County Archives.*

This page, bottom: Dump truck on scale—this truck scale is now a garden. *Croton Historical Society.*

Opposite: Capping of the landfill, circa 1991. *Croton Historical Society.*

Then engineers covered it all with a geotextile to prevent rainwater from percolating through the waste and built an elaborate system of wells and piping to manage the byproducts of all this organic material.

Ideas on how to utilize the newly capped landfill were varied—ranging from a golf course to a tilapia fish farm, the latter heated with methane generated by the decomposing pile. Viewed from Park Headquarters today, this wildflower-covered hill presents a benign scene. An "artificial" grassland (so called because it will never be allowed to progress into a woodland,) it provides a static niche ecosystem. And with its elevation creating a bump for the prevailing northwesterly wind, it is common to see raptors kiting, hanging motionless in the air, while searching for prey in the point's rodent-rich environment.

In 1996, when the Westchester County Executive held a press conference on the newly capped landfill, Riverkeeper, in a positive spirit befitting that day, proclaimed that "we are dancing on the grave of a monster."[52] Unfortunately, we can't just bury our problems and forget them. This capped landfill is more like a tiger in a cage than a grave, with maintenance requirements far more complex and the beast within far more dangerous.

Officially designated a Class 2 Inactive Hazardous Waste disposal site, this is critical infrastructure. Engineered and expensive, it is a 24-hour, 365-day mitigation machine. This seemingly harmless mound has 5.5 miles of piping and 113 wells that extract leachate as well as methane gas that is constantly being produced by the decaying material. These materials will forever be reminding us of the stewardship required to responsibly manage the result of society's progress.

THE FUTURE

To some degree, local environmentalists and the staff who maintain the landfill have become victims of their own success. When the landfill was active, it didn't take a whole lot of imagination to realize what a hazard it was: gulls circling over the growing pile of garbage, a seemingly endless line of noisy smelly trucks rumbling along Croton Point Avenue and the landscape of rusting fifty-five-gallon drums and bulldozers creeping over this mountain of trash created a scene straight out of a horror film. It was relatively easy to get to get folks mobilized to advocate for change against this backdrop.

Today, the potential threats to the point are more subtle but just as dangerous as before—from invasive species to chemicals invisibly seeping into the river. Both require expertise and expense to identify as well as mitigate but are difficult to dramatize in a slick meme or media campaign.

Today, Croton Point serves a dual role in the Hudson River Environmental movement. On one hand, the point had been a fertile ground for creating all kinds of environmentalists. On the other hand, it is an unquestioned environmental victory, and the ongoing mitigation requiring constant vigilance and funding will always serve as a reminder of the far-reaching implications of our actions.

In 2015, more than $600,000 of federal and state funds were secured to help remediate the landfill meadow. When the renowned landscape architect Larry Weiner spoke about the landfill, he might have been speaking about the entire point when he said, "The Croton grassland, as a former landfill, is also a symbolic landscape, a 100-acre manifestation of humanity's potential to restore habitat and create something of lasting value and beauty."[53]

———◇◈◇———

ENVIRONMENTAL CHRONOLOGY

1923

Westchester County buys Croton Point to develop into a park and establishes a small municipal dump on seventy acres.

1924

Croton Point Park officially opens.

1962

Con Edison announces plans build a pump storage facility in Storm King Mountain, the same day that Rachel Carson's *Silent Spring* is published (September 27).

1963

Scenic Hudson is formed in response to the Storm King Proposal.

1966

Hudson River Fisherman's Association (HRFA) holds first public meeting at the American Legion in Crotonville.

1970

First Earth Day.

1972

Federal court orders landfill to be phased out.

1980

Storm King settlement is reached; Con Edison is prevented from building its facility there.

1986

Croton Landfill closes.

HRFA and Riverkeeper merge.

1993

Landfill capping is completed.

———◇◈◇———

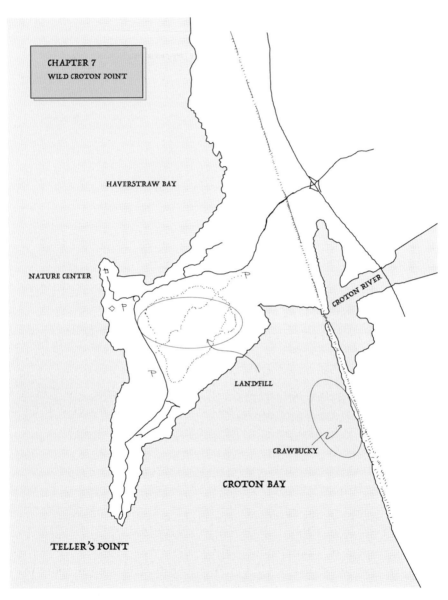

CHAPTER 7
WILD CROTON POINT

HAVERSTRAW BAY

NATURE CENTER

CROTON RIVER

LANDFILL

CRAWBUCKY

CROTON BAY

TELLER'S POINT

Sketch map of Wild Croton Point. *Map by Harrison Isaac.*

Chapter 7

WILD CROTON POINT

Nature is a wet place where large numbers of ducks fly overhead uncooked.
—Oscar Wilde

Croton Point has long been an ideal location to watch, learn about and interact with nature. Situated along a major flyway, next to an ever-changing salt front and at the apex of a natural fishing trap, the number of species of fish, birds and mammals recorded here is stunning. Just as important are the local naturalists and nature organizations that generously share their knowledge and resources with the public.

FEATHERS

With the advent of the Internet, crowd-sourced websites like the Cornell Lab of Ornithology's Ebird.org and the *Hudson Valley Almanac*, compiled by the Department of Conservation (DEC), allow easy access to the sharing and finding of information. Croton Point currently features in more than ten thousand online "bird checklists" that have been compiled by birders and citizen scientists on E-bird.

Even on a bitterly cold weekday in February, it is common to find at least a dozen folks on the landfill with bazooka-like lenses, all focused on finding the latest "accidental" reported online. (An "accidental" or a "vagrant" is a bird

Croton Point grasslands. *Photo by Bonnie Coe.*

seen outside of its normal range.) Local experts have seen sandhill cranes, snowy owls, LeConte sparrows and golden eagles, with local rare bird expert Michael Bochnik speculating that the rarest bird ever seen on the point was the yellow-billed albatross of 1976.

By far the most popular bird on the point is the American bald eagle ("bald" is short for "piebald," meaning brown and white). Bald eagles primarily feed on fish, and they need open water to find this essential food source. While eagles inhabit the northern climes during the summer months, they are compelled to fly south during the coldest months to find open water. Historically, the river could and did freeze all the way across, but these days the Coast Guard will no longer allow that to happen, as it must maintain the channel for oil to be barged up to Albany. Because of this, no matter how cold it gets, the Hudson River around the point remains open and has become a popular spot for seeing eagles.

Between 1860 and 1960, there were only 72 nests recorded in New York State, and shooting eagles was encouraged. In 1972, with only one nesting pair documented in New York State, the pesticide DDT was banned, and a

Above: A mature American bald eagle. *Photo by Bonnie Coe.*

Left: Teatown EagleFest poster. *Teatown Lake Reservation.*

A flying mature American bald eagle. *Photo by Bonnie Coe.*

An immature American bald eagle enjoying lunch. *Photo by Bonnie Coe.*

> ### HUDSON RIVER ALMANAC
>
> A weekly "insiders" report on what people are seeing along the river, the *Hudson River Almanac* is a terrific combination of science and crowdsourcing. Compiled and distributed by the DEC, and with nearly twenty thousand subscribers, it is one of our favorite weekly reads. We highly encourage people to subscribe and contribute. *www.dec.ny.gov.*

year later, the American bald eagle was classified as endangered. It took the likes of Rachel Carson on a national level, plus New York DEC's Peter Nye, to bring this magnificent bird back to the valley. Between 1976 and 1989, 198 eagles were captured in Alaska and released in New York State. As of 2017, the annual DEC eagle census confirmed that there are 426 occupied nesting sites in the state, a rare, remarkable triumph in the world of endangered species and Hudson River Valley's most visible example of local "regreening."

Largely due to this resurgence in the eagle population, since the early 2000s, local nature preserve Teatown Reservation has sponsored an EagleFest on Croton Point in early February. Started by local New York City Fire Department captain Charlie Roberto, EagleFest has introduced thousands of people to these iconic raptors and allowed many people to see eagles in the wild for the first time. With plenty of sponsors, the fest has become the de facto midwinter gathering for many disparate groups that care about the local environment.

Today, birders take for granted the plethora of birds that circle and swoop over the Hudson Valley: eagles, ravens, hawks and even black vultures are now commonplace. In fact, eagles and hawks are now routinely seen all along the Hudson today, even as far south as Midtown Manhattan.

THE MODERN BIRDING MOVEMENT

It is no exaggeration to say that Croton Point played an integral role in creating the modern birding movement. Some might associate the beginning of bird study in America with John James Audubon and his epic book *The Birds of America*, first published in 1827. Audubon's systematic study of every bird in North America and artistic color images was groundbreaking...and big. In attempting to draw life-sized birds, he had to print them on "double elephant folio" size paper, even then having to place some of the larger birds in odd poses to fit. At the time, the study of birds usually involved a shotgun and the preparation of "study skins" (basically two-dimensional taxidermy). No one else was engraving copper plates or hand-coloring the images like this, much less publishing them.

In a bit of serendipity for our story, the engraver for Audubon's opus was one John J. Havell Jr. He could see Croton Point from his house high up on a hill in what was then called Sing Sing (now Ossining.) But even though both Audubon and Havell lived in the lower Hudson River Valley, it would take a young art student from a small upstate town, inspired while counting birds on Croton Point, to change birding forever and start an environmental movement.

ROGER TORY PETERSON

Roger Tory Peterson was born in 1908 in Jamestown, New York. A talented artist, he spent his formative years exploring the local backwoods of Jamestown with an endlessly curious mind about the natural wonders around him. But when an opportunity to study art in New York City came around, he took it. Joining the Bronx County Bird Club, he participated in the annual Christmas Count on Croton Point, and a chance conversation occurred there that sparked the modern birding and environmental movements.

The annual Christmas Count was a relatively new idea, evolving from the Annual Christmas Shoot. Started in 1900, it was a systematic local census of birds conducted once a year meant to act as a long-term barometer of local bird populations. Today, this count has been joined by "The Big Day" in May, sponsored by the Audubon Society and E-bird. These yearly recorded sightings, along with many other such efforts, are the kind of crowd-sourced citizen science that has been instrumental in illustrating national and global trends like climate change and habitat destruction.

> *I consider myself the bridge between the shotgun and the binoculars in bird watching. Before I came along, the primary way to observe birds was to shoot them and stuff them.*
>
> —*Roger Tory Peterson*

All you need, thanks to Roger Tory Peterson. *Photo by Scott Craven.*

Peterson had a genius for boiling things down and used a series of field marks to identify birds. In his sketches, he grouped birds together from the same family, in the same pose, and used small arrows to point out the unique physical cues that could easily be seen with binoculars. He understood that the average person was not going to look at study skins or have the ability or time to draw birds in the field.

This innovative method led to the publication of the first field guide for the general public—Peterson's *A Field Guide to the Birds*. Originally published in 1934, it was an instant success. The gateway book for generations of environmentalists, it enabled anyone to pick up a pair of binoculars, stick a little book in their pocket, walk outside and start to understand.

Over the years, more field guides covering everything from mushrooms to stars were published, expanding the knowledge base and provoking interest in the outdoors. And it all began on Croton Point.

FINS

Croton Point sits in the middle of two discrete sections of the river that hold a tremendous variety of marine life. The birds are well aware of this, hence the plethora of eagles, cormorants, belted kingfishers and great blue herons that come to eat these fish. As of this writing there have been 236 species of fishes documented in the Hudson River, of which 75 percent are native.[54]

Left: Striped bass—this little guy is going back in the water. *Photo by Scott Craven.*

Above: NYS road sign. *Photo by Scott Craven.*

The headline species are those fish that live in both salt and fresh water, such as the Atlantic sturgeon, the striped bass, the American shad and the blueback herring. The only species found in the Hudson that live most of their lives in fresh water, returning to salt to breed, are the common eel and the blue crab.

Of all these fishes, the Atlantic sturgeon is the icon of the Hudson. With its picture adorning every Hudson River Tributary road sign, this powerful symbol is seen by thousands, if not millions in the valley every year.

An ancient, primitive fish, the sturgeon is a scaleless (they have plates called "scutes"), cartilaginous fish (no real bones, like a shark). A benthic cruiser that swims along the bottom looking for food, sturgeon are renowned for their roe as caviar. They can also be eaten pickled or smoked and are put in chowder (where they are said to have an almost pork-like mouthfeel). In the nineteenth century, they were so commonly eaten in the valley that they were referred to as "Albany Beef."[55]

With an unusual habit of leaping out of the water, they are one of the few fish the casual observer can sometimes see from Croton Point. And they can get astonishingly big—in 2018, University of Delaware geology professor John Madsen was studying the bottom of the river with a high-definition side-scan sonar when, to his surprise, he found a living, fourteen-foot sturgeon cruising on the bottom. Its weight was estimated at more than eight hundred pounds and age at about ninety years old, bigger than any sturgeon previously recorded in the Hudson River.

HENRY GOURDINE

Henry Gourdine was a legendary figure on the Hudson River. Born on Croton Point in 1903, his father worked in the Underhill brickyards as an engineer for the small-gauge steam train used to move bricks around the point. Henry had vivid memories of the lively workings of the brickworks, and how his father would let him ring the bell to call the workers every morning.

By the 1920s, he had a lucrative fishing business off Ossining, and his skill set included making his own boats and nets. He witnessed rumrunners, deadly prison breaks and epic hauls of fish from the waters around Croton Point. Experiencing the vagaries of the industry, Henry worked as a carpenter while raising a family and seasonally fishing. Although his expertise was renowned—he was known as the "Net Doctor" for his prowess in making and repairing nets—it was his character that made him stand out to a generation of folks trying to understand the river more deeply.

Henry Gourdine was a generous mentor, a storyteller and a nonchalant guardian of the river. With his slow, self-effacing style, Henry would chuckle and talk about the old-timers he knew with anyone who was smart enough to listen. He was able to pass on his insider's knowledge of the Hudson River— its bottom, tides, currents and seasonal moods—to a new generation. They continue to carry on his traditions and stewardship.

When he passed away in 1997 at the age of ninety-four, Governor Pataki proclaimed that Henry Gourdine was "a state treasure." The community of Ossining felt the same way and named its new waterfront park, that stands where Henry's fishing shack one stood, after this extraordinary man.

Left: Henry Gourdine's nets drying on the Ossining Waterfront. *Ossining Historical Society.*

Right: Henry Gourdine fishing on the Hudson. *Ossining Historical Society.*

The original inhabitants of the point had been depending on, and harvesting, both fin fish and shellfish for thousands of years. Catching fish in traps called weirs, with nets and with spears, evidence of this fishery has left us some of our oldest traces of human occupation here in the form of shell middens and stone tools.

The first Europeans in the valley established commercial fisheries on and around Croton Point, and the piscine star of this era was the American shad. The largest member of the herring family, the shad were an integral part of Hudson River culture, with planked shad festivals in the spring and the ability to clean these notoriously bony fish considered a legendary superpower.

Local fisherman would set fixed nets, called "shots," perpendicular to the bank to catch shad. Every spring when the shad would migrate up the Hudson River to spawn, local men who worked a variety of other trades during the rest of the year would come together to retrieve the saplings that had been stored all winter under the water and pound them into the soft bottom of the river, stretching gill nets across. If you stood on the southern tip of the point in the spring, there would have been row after row of saplings sticking out of the water as far down the east bank as you could see.

These fish and their roe were either sold locally or, in the twentieth century, brought down to the Fulton Fish Market. (Fisherman on the south side of Ossining would keep their catch alive in flooded nineteenth-century copper mines until they had enough to bring down to the market.)

Another type of commercial fishing practiced on the point involved seines, sometimes more than two thousand feet long. These nets, with weights on the bottom and floats on the top, corralled fish onto the beach. Large windlasses called "crabs" or "reels" were sunk into the shore along the south side of Croton Point, as well as on Crawbuckie Point across the Croton Bay. (Crawbuckie Point was a sandy point on the south side of the mouth of the Croton River, formed by sand transported by the river up the Ossining shoreline. It was "starved" out of existence in the 1980s when the Ossining waterfront was repaired and modernized.)

Sadly, in 1996, due to diminishing stocks of fish, New York State officially prohibited both commercial and recreational shad fishing in the Hudson. Also, in 1996, all fishing for sturgeon was outlawed, with a forty-year moratorium imposed in New York and other Atlantic states.

As of October 2021, there are several health advisories in place around Croton Point. With concerns about legacy contaminants such as PCBs, dioxins and cadmium, consumption of fish from the Hudson is severely

---

BOOTLEGGERS OFF THE POINT

During Prohibition, bootleggers bringing alcohol up the Hudson River were often pursued by federal authorities off Croton Point. Hoping to avoid capture, they would jettison their crates of alcohol over the side. Always hating to see things go to waste, the local fishermen would drag the crates up the next day with fishing nets. Legend has it that in order to bring the booze down to New York to sell, it was a bottle to every patrolman and two to every sergeant in Ossining to get out of town.

---

restricted. Please check the current advisories before even considering eating what you catch.[56]

Today, the only fishing that happens off Croton Point is for sport, and the fishermen are as varied and diverse as the fish. Standing atop the landfill in the spring, you can look to the south over Croton Bay and see a flotilla of small craft. To the north, larger boats are required out in Haverstraw Bay. With the shallower Croton Bay warming up the earliest, this spot is an early season favorite for catching striped bass.

These fish have been caught in increasingly large sizes. Currently, dedicated anglers are catching female striped bass, commonly called "cows," weighing more than fifty pounds, every year. Getting a thirty-inch striper off Croton Point no longer guarantees that your Polaroid will end up on the refrigerator in the local bait and tackle store.

Other popular fish found off the point include the common carp. Introduced in the early 1800s and considered "garbage fish," fishermen used to shoot these gigantic minnows with bows and arrows, as it was thought that these invasive carp were destroying the eggs of the local sports fish. In the early part of the twentieth century, carp were caught off the point and then sold in the city as a popular ingredient in gefilte fish.

With an array of expensive rods and dough balls created with a take-to-your-grave recipe, modern anglers have made carp fishing an art. And carp are the perfect fish for those who don't want to take them home and eat them—these enormous fish make the perfect "grip and grin" selfie to share with all your friends on social media.

Arguably, the most important type of fishing currently going on off the point involves wader-clad river educators. These dedicated men and women are harvesting and creating the valley's most important catch: a new generation of environmentalists who care about the river.

Commonly seen on the sandy north side of the point, they use a seine to capture jellyfish-like "combs," YOY (young of the year) striped bass, eels and an endless array of assorted fish. Hauls onto the beach always bring excitement and expectation.

Scoop a little fish out of a bucket, hold it in the palm of your hand and then watch it swim away when you put it back. Experiencing this in the same body of water seen every day, now it's not the fish that are caught—it's the kids. If you ever see some kids staring into a bucket on the beach, walk over, join them and engage with the incredible variety of this river's fish bounty.

FUR

As far as our furry friends are concerned, the point plays host to the usual suspects in this part of southeastern New York: white-tailed deer, fox and squirrel. Mink are occasionally seen, and even the elusive fisher has been observed. In the early 1990s, there was even a rare piebald deer on the point.

Another group of mammals that are back in the valley are the marine ones. In 2006, a wandering manatee showed up for a month in Haverstraw Bay. And seeing seals hauled out on rocks, especially in the winter, is no longer that unusual—the *Hudson River Almanac* regularly documents them. After they are tagged and traced, our ability to follow the travels of these animals make their presence here even more fascinating.

DON'T FEED (SOME OF) THE ANIMALS

One of the consequences of the regreening of the Hudson Valley is learning how to live responsibly with reintroduced and thriving animal populations. It is an ever-present challenge for modern suburbia. One thing you should never do is feed a wild animal. Although well intentioned, feeding habituates these animals to people and teaches them to aggressively seek food, ultimately becoming a dangerous nuisance. The expression out west for years has been "A fed bear is a dead bear." Do our local animals a favor and don't feed them.

Eastern coyote on Croton Point. *Photo by Bonnie Coe.*

One of the newcomers to the point is the eastern coyote, an animal that didn't even exist until the twentieth century. After the destruction of the Plains buffalo herds in the nineteenth century, coyotes expanded east. Passing through southern Ontario before dropping into New York State across the St. Lawrence River in the 1920s, they picked up a little wolf and domesticated dog DNA on the way. Now considered a hybrid species,

---

MAXIMUM SECURITY PINNIPEDS (AKA SEALS)

On a particularly cold, clear day in 1993, a sharp-eyed tower guard on one of Sing Sing's river posts saw a small object on one of the ice floes drifting down with the outgoing tide from Croton Point. As it got closer, it became obvious that it was a seal. Concerned for the motionless animal, the officer called the police, and soon there were several police cars and the fire department on the waterfront preparing to launch a boat in an attempt to "rescue" the seal. Fortunately, calmer heads prevailed, the fire department was canceled and as the seal floated by, it lifted its head and looked at the police cars with haughty disdain before it putting its head back down and dozing off again. All agreed that if the seal had been behaving normally, like balancing a ball on its nose, no one would have been concerned in the first place.

---

they are most often seen on or around the landfill at dawn or dusk. Masters of adaptation, they have spread to all the lower forty-eight states and have even been seen in Manhattan.

INVADERS

One of the wonders of today's Croton Point is the opportunity to try and picture what it looked like before the heavy hand of settlement and industrialization. As Croton Point offers a microcosmic view of the valley, many of the issues it faces mirror those of the Hudson Valley at large.

Many of the birds, plants, even fish that we catch—elements we have always considered everyday parts of our natural ecosystem—were not present when the Europeans first arrived. New avenues into the valley created by our modern society—like ballast water in ships, the Erie Canal and deliberate introduction—have been supplying a steady stream of these nonnative animals and plants from around the globe. This is compounded by global climate change, which has made the ranges of many species more dynamic than they have ever been.

Some examples include swans, largemouth bass, starlings (because if they were mentioned in Shakespeare, America should have some) spotted lanternflys and the terrifyingly named northern snakehead—none was here when Hudson sailed up the river in 1609.

Yet it's one of the most seemingly benign and ubiquitous species on the point that is the signature invasive: the common reed. Standing on the landfill today and looking south to Ossining, one sees tall, densely compacted and seemingly impenetrable tall grasses along the shore. This is the same expanse of light-brown reeds that spreads all over the mouth of the Croton River when you look out at the point while crossing the 9A bridge—they've become part of our everyday landscape and backdrop.

These reeds are *Phragmites australis*. Part of a larger global family of reeds, they are related to a species native to North America, but it's the plants from Europe that have spread throughout the lower valley over the last fifty years. While they threaten biodiversity and choke out native species, such as cattails and spartina grass, it has also been argued that *Phragmites* buffer communities from storm surges better than the original species. Either way, the question of what to do with these particular invasives is almost an academic one, as their removal is so labor intensive and so many others present a much more immediate danger (snakeheads, zebra mussels, hydrilla) that addressing these reeds on the point is low on the list of priorities. While one of the wonders

Invasive *Phragmites* on south beach of Croton Point. *Photo by Scott Craven.*

of the point is its accessible representation of so many of the larger themes in the valley, we all could live without this one.

Seals "hauled" out on rocks in the winter, striped bass surging into Croton Bay, eastern coyotes howling at night and invasive plants extending their rhizomes through the mud—Croton Point represents our intimate, long-standing relationship with the wild world in the Hudson Valley.

In 2018, for the first time in decades, maybe even a century, eagles were born on Croton Point.

———⟨◆⟩———

WILD CROTON POINT CHRONOLOGY

1851
"A shark of the shovel-nosed species measuring eight and a half feet in length and weighing an estimated three hundred pounds, was taken at Croton Cove."[57]

1926
"Mrs. Gillespie, the superintendent's wife, had barnyard hens hatch Ring-necked pheasant eggs she acquired from the Conservation Commission. The thirty pheasants would then respond to be fed when Mrs. Gillespie blew her police whistle at 5:00PM every day."[58]

1930s
Famed local fisherman Henry Gourdine takes twelve thousand pounds of fish in a single haul.

1961
Constructing a new highway ramp for the Taconic nearby at Route 134, workers uncover a femur bone from a woolly mammoth, providing evidence that these giant hairy elephants roamed the area sometime after the last glacier receded up the valley.

1972

Only one nesting eagle site is documented in all of New York State.

2006

A manatee is seen repeatedly during the month of August in Haverstraw Bay. Named "Tappie," she disappears and was hoped to have returned to warmer climes.

2012

A harbor seal is seen "hauled out" on the rocks of Enoch's Point.

2017

426 nesting eagle sites are documented in New York State.

2018

The first eagle is born on Croton Point in decades.

———◇※◇———

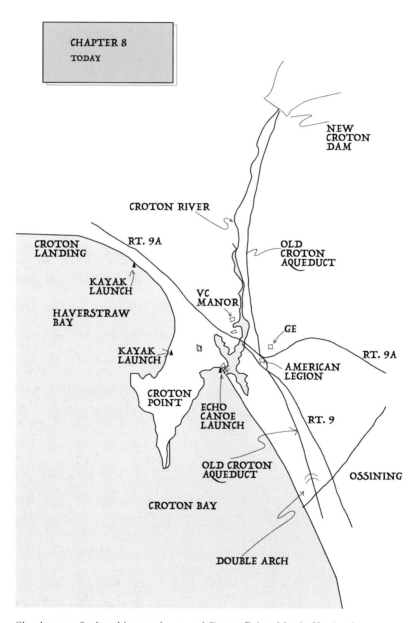

NEW
CROTON
DAM

CROTON RIVER

CROTON
LANDING

RT. 9A

OLD
CROTON
AQUEDUCT

KAYAK
LAUNCH

VC
MANOR

HAVERSTRAW
BAY

GE

KAYAK
LAUNCH

RT. 9A

AMERICAN
LEGION

CROTON
POINT

ECHO
CANOE
LAUNCH

RT. 9

OLD CROTON
AQUEDUCT

OSSINING

CROTON BAY

DOUBLE ARCH

Sketch map of other things to do around Croton Point. *Map by Harrison Isaac.*

Chapter 8

OTHER THINGS TO DO

Although we feel that Croton Point is the best thing to see in the area, it is also a good jumping-off site for the Hudson Valley explorer, with several different things to see and ways to see them.

BIKING

Give a man a fish and feed him for a day, teach a man to fish and feed him for a lifetime. Teach a man to cycle and he will realize fishing is stupid and boring.

—Desmond Tutu

When we talk about "bikes," we're talking about hybrid bikes, gravel bikes and preferably mountain bikes. As of this writing, Metro North railroad has a program for bringing bikes on the train during certain times—check its website. Also, biking the point is a great way to see it—just stay on the designated roads and trails. (No fat biking on Mother's Lap!)

HIKING

The truth reveals itself to those who travel on foot.

—Werner Herzog

Ventilation tower on the Old Croton Aqueduct. *Photo by Scott Craven.*

When we talk about hiking, we're not talking about crampons and ice axes hiking, we're talking about sturdy shoes and bug repellent hiking. (Any responsible person spending time in nature in the Northeast should conduct a thorough tick check afterward. Tick-borne illnesses are no joke.)

South to the Old Croton Aqueduct and then North to Croton Dam (Approx. 9-Mile Round Trip)

About twenty years ago, when they were overhauling Route 9 between Croton and Ossining, the engineers made sure to put in a guarded bike path. Awkwardly named the "Crossining" (Croton + Ossining + river crossing), although no one calls it that, it is a great, safe connector. Before the state put this walkway in, you would have risked your life attempting to either walk or bike between the two communities.

Take this bike path south from the point (entrance is next to the Route 9 South entrance ramp). After crossing the Croton River, there's a slight uphill to the traffic light. At the light, cross Route 9 to Old Albany Post Road. You'll pass the Parker-Bale American Legion Hall on your left, the site of the meeting that created the Hudson River Fisherman's Association, before you

Spillway of the New Croton Dam. *Photo by Scott Craven.*

New Croton Dam. *Photo by Scott Craven.*

FRIENDS OF THE OLD CROTON AQUEDUCT

A group dedicated to the Old Croton Aqueduct, Friends has been instrumental in advocating for and promoting this gem. With work parties, tours and information, it has gotten this long-ignored, wonderful piece of history the attention it deserves. We highly recommend it and any of its numerous events and tours. *Aqueduct.org.*

pass under the Route 9A bridge. After the bridge, the GE Global Learning Crotonville Campus will be on your right. Stay on Old Albany Post Road, riding uphill until you take a right onto Samstag Avenue (probably named after Philip Samstag, the Croton Point winedresser). You'll soon make a right onto Hillcrest Avenue (it's okay to walk your bike here; we have, and one of us was a bike cop here). After "summiting" Hillcrest, it's a downhill glide to the entrance to the Old Croton Aqueduct trail, marked by a sign and several large blocks of stone across the front.

Traveling north for the next two miles, you will be on a flat, well-maintained trail that is built on top of the old 1842 aqueduct. You will cross a few roads and go through a rock cut and under some power lines before emerging at the New Croton Dam, all while being relatively shaded and with the constant companion of the Croton River below you on your left.

If you have never seen the New Croton Dam before, you will be awestruck. Completed in 1906, it is more than 250 feet across at its base and almost 300 feet high. When it was completed, it was the tallest dam in the world and was considered to be the second-largest cut-stone structure in the world, second only to the great pyramids.

You can bike/walk across the top of the dam to the other side to see the one-thousand-foot-long spillway, and if water is coming over the top, it's something you will not soon forget. If you remember, take a moment to think about the folks, mostly immigrants, who built this dam and the rest of this incredible system. This critical part of our infrastructure is one of the first parts of the system that has provided us with clean drinking water, the likes of which many in the world have never had, for almost two centuries.

South to the Old Croton Aqueduct, then South to the Double Arches (Approx. 5-Mile Round Trip)

Take the same bike path as above across the Croton River to the first stop light. However, instead of making the left, keep going south; halfway up the first little hill, you'll see the entrance to the Old Croton Aqueduct on the right. You will travel south through some condos, across several roads, and you'll even negotiate some stairs before finding yourself at Ossining's Weir Chamber (if you're lucky, Friends of the Old Croton Aqueduct will be conducting a tour and you can access the inside of this 1842 water tube).

Continue on and you'll be on top of Ossining's famous Double Arches. At this spot, the builders of the aqueduct carried the water, at its constant slight decline, over the Sing Sing Kill. Look over the edge; below, you'll see another arch carrying a roadway through the larger arch—pretty odd.

After crossing the arch, turn left, down and across to the Ossining Community Center; if the museum is open, check out the Aqueduct/Sing Sing Prison Museum. Cross the parking lot and go down the ramp to the Sing Sing Kill walkway. Newly completed, it takes you under the Double Arches for a great perspective. (If it looks familiar, it was in a scene of Spike Lee's 2018 movie *BlacKkKlansman*.)

Ossining Double Arches, as seen from the Sing Sing Kill walkway. *Photo by Scott Craven.*

LAW AND (DIS)ORDER, PART 1

September 17, 1926. The steamship *Martha* was hired by a group of people looking to get away up the Hudson; they were dropped off in Peekskill for the day. On the return trip, it became obvious to the captain that his passengers had spent the day drinking, so when a fight broke out, he pulled the ship to the dock at Verplanck and went ashore to seek help. Seizing this opportunity, the inebriated ne'er-do-wells threw the crew overboard and forced the pilot to leave the dock and head south down the river. Ultimately, they forced the pilot to run the ship on to the bathing beach at Croton Point to make their escape. Sadly, in the ensuing mad scramble to flee the ship, at least one person lost their life. It is unknown if the subsequent investigation ever identified any individual involved.

Retrace your steps and get back on to the aqueduct, where you can head south a short distance to Ossining's Main Street Crescent, where there are all types of food. When you're done, you can retrace your route back to the point or just go down the hill to Ossining's Metro North train station.

To Croton Landing Park (Approx. 4-Mile Round Trip)

Before you enter Croton Point Park, across from the ball field, on your right you'll find a hike/bike trail that leads north. Winding itself for about a mile between the railroad yards and a condo complex, the path will bring you along the Hudson River. Traveling north, over land that held several brickyards and boatyards in the nineteenth century, you'll ride about another mile to the 9/11 memorial. With a sweeping vista of Haverstraw Bay with a great perspective of Croton Point to the south, this is one of the great view sheds of the lower river valley, as well as a very popular walking path.

VAN CORTLANDT MANOR

Just up Croton Point Avenue and then down to the right on South Riverside, Van Cortlandt Manor is geologically part of Croton Point itself. One of the crown jewels of Historic Hudson Valley's many sites, this beautifully preserved and well-maintained seventeenth-century manor house is a great

North end of Croton Landing Park, with Croton Point in distance. *Photo by Scott Craven.*

Van Cortlandt Manor. *Photo Scott Craven.*

way to gain insight into the valley's history through the centuries-old story of one of the valley's most prominent families. Although better known these days for its iconic Halloween Pumpkin "Blaze," it is sometimes still open for tours as a historical site. *Hudsonvalley.org.*

CROTON HISTORICAL SOCIETY

The Croton Historical Society is located in the Croton Municipal Building at 1 Van Wyck Street, Croton-on-Hudson. If anything you have seen on the point, at the Croton Dam or even regarding the brick industry has piqued your interest, a pilgrimage to the historical society is a must. With a strong online presence combined with a well-organized and zealously staffed physical collection, it's the final word on Croton history. *Crotonhistoricalsociety.org.*

LAW AND (DIS)ORDER, PART 2

April 11, 1988. It was early on a quiet Sunday morning when a store clerk in Stamford, Connecticut, confronted a man shoplifting. Taking out a sawed-off shotgun, he took the clerk hostage and fled in a vehicle, ultimately leading the police on a two-state, Blues Brothers–style vehicle pursuit, ultimately ending on Croton Point.

Apparently, the perp had not read the first chapter of his *How to Elude the Police* handbook or he would have known that turning on to a long point, surrounded by water, hoping to get away from the fuzz, is, as they say, tactically unsound. He compounded his bad decision-making by a firing a shot at the police as he skidded to a halt, crawled into the river and started swimming across the Hudson.

The Ossining police, who had been listening to the whole thing on the radio, responded to the waterfront and "borrowed" a boat. They were soon able to scoop up the perp as he struggled to swim to Rockland County under the hovering state police helicopter.

Croton Point Nature Center. *Photo by Scott Craven.*

CROTON POINT NATURE CENTER

If your historical interests run more toward the original inhabitants, the place to go is the Croton Point Nature Center. Located on Enoch's Point, it is usually open on weekends during the season. With an impressive collection of artifacts, the naturalist and the archaeological society that calls this spot home are the local experts in this rapidly evolving research. Anyone really interested in pursuing this should contact and follow the Louis A. Brennan, Lower Hudson Chapter of the New York State Archaeological Association. *Lablhc.org.*

KAYAK/PADDLE

Wherever there is a channel for water, there is a road for the canoe.
—Henry David Thoreau

Local paddling is experiencing a boom. With three hand launches available nearby, many visitors to the area are finding the perspective from the water the best of all. One of these launches is on Croton Point itself. Located behind Park Headquarters, the park hand launch is a great access to the north and Haverstraw Bay. However, it is condition-dependent. If the wind is from the northwest, as it often is, both the park launch and the second launch at Croton Landing Park are at the wrong end of a long fetch of water. After blowing over the widest, shallowest spot on the Hudson River, the wind can make the water here too rough. Exercise caution, be prepared and remember that you always have other options for launching, including staying on shore sipping coffee. (If the kite surfers are flying fifteen feet in the air north of the point, that is a good indication it might not be such great idea to go paddling.)

The third hand launch in the area is the Echo Canoe Launch, named after Theodore Cornu's environmental movement. South of the Croton-Harmon railroad station, near the salt shed, there is a great place to launch if the wind is blowing out of the northwest and the other two launches are unsafe. Although relatively sheltered from any northwest wind, enjoyable use of this location is dependent on the tides.

Tides in this portion of the Hudson vary by about three feet. In the Hudson River, there are usually two high tides and two low tides per day. The best thing about tides is that they are predictable, and the tide schedules are easily accessible—a cursory check on the Internet will allow you to view

Echo Canoe Launch, mouth of the Croton River. *Photo by Scott Craven.*

PADDLING SAFETY

The Croton River has become an extremely popular place for small, hand-powered craft. An incredible array of kayaks, sit-on-top kayaks, SUPs (stand-up paddleboards) and even skin-on-frame Adirondack guide boats ply these waters. It's a great place for all of them. However, all of us should exercise caution. *Always* wear your Personal Floatation Device ("lifejacket") even if you're a good swimmer—it makes a huge difference. The Croton River can be unpredictably cold, with occasional releases from the bottom of the Croton Dam. Even in the middle of the summer, the water can be "refreshing." Even a great swimmer can struggle if suddenly immersed in cold water. We highly recommend that if you are going to pursue this sport, please take a lesson from one of several outfitters here in the valley. See you on the river!

tides months in advance. A rising tide is a great time for a trip up the tidal portion of the Croton River. Turning up the Croton River and traveling under Route 9, historical spots, wildlife and a beautiful deep gorge await you in this hidden gem. It's one of our favorite spots in the whole world (don't tell anyone!).

If you launch and choose to go under the railroad bridge toward the Hudson River, you can access the southern portion of Croton Point. You will have a great paddle one mile out to Teller's Point and back without ever exposing yourself to the northwest wind. Just be judicious and stop shy of the extreme tip, with its swirling currents and gravel reef.

However, if the tide is rising, be mindful of the fact that if you time it wrong, you might have difficulty fitting under the bridge on the way back. Remember, *never, ever* try to walk across the railroad tracks; it is illegal and dangerous, with its electrified third rails and four busy tracks. If on your return to the launch you find your access back under the railroad bridge blocked by the tide, you can always wait it out or just paddle down to the public launch on the Ossining waterfront and hop a train back to your car.

In season, there is often a kayak rental concession based out of Echo Launch. The Croton Recreation Department also rents out kayak seasonal storage (preference to residents). Check with the rec department for updated info on either of these programs. *Crotononhudson-ny.gov.*

SUNDRIES

Despite the fact that Croton Point is a busy park, it has few if any regular concessions. Fortunately, plenty of provisions are a quick walk, bike or drive nearby. Leaving the park, travel under Route 9 and keep going up Croton Point Avenue until intersects with South Riverside Avenue at the light. On your right, down the hill, you'll see a large supermarket, and on your left, up the hill, you'll find a bakery, among other things, for your provisions.

CHRONOLOGY RELATING TO OTHER THINGS TO DO
1841
The almost completed Croton Dam (the original, not the one we see today) bursts after three days of drenching rain on top of snow. The Croton River becomes a wall of water and debris as it rushes five miles to the Hudson River, dumping tons of sediment at the mouth and forever changing the character of the river in the shadow of the point.

1842
Water enters the original Croton Aqueduct for the first time, reaching the receiving reservoir, where the New York Public Library stands today, twenty-two hours later.

1890s
For several years, American Canoe Association holds its annual meeting on the point.

1968
Old Croton Aqueduct Park is created.

1993
The "Crossining" is completed.

1990s
Croton Landing Park is completed.

NOTES

Preface

1. Westchester County Records, Liber A (182), in Horecky, "Ft. Kitchawanc Archeological Preserve"; Bolton, "History of the County of Westchester," 36.

Chapter 1

2. Titus and Titus, *Hudson Valley in the Ice Age*, 194.

Chapter 2

3. Brennan, "Lower Hudson: A Decade of Shell Middens," 81.
4. Pickman, "Cultural Resources Survey, Croton Point Park," 21.
5. Bolton, "History of the County of Westchester," 114.
6. Scharf, *History of Westchester County*, 234.
7. Harrington, Report Concerning Archeological Investigations, Appendix A.
8. Stockbridge-Munsee Cultural Affairs Department, communications with the author, January, 2022.
9. Fiedel, "Archaic and Woodland Occupations at Teller's Point," 10.
10. Juet, *Juet's Journal of Hudson's 1609 Voyage*, 586.
11. Van der Donck, Gehring and Starna, *Description of New Netherland*, 53.
12. Stockbridge-Munsee Band of Mohican Indians Resource Guide.
13. Jacobs, *New Netherland*, 135.
14. Van Lear, Documents Relating to New Netherland, 4:279–80.
15. Westchester Deeds, Liber A, February 4, 1682, 181.

Chapter 3

16. There's even a memorial to this event called the Boot Monument at the Saratoga National Park, https://www.nps.gov/places/boot-monument.htm.
17. Philbrick, *Valiant Ambition*, 259.
18. Schonnard and Spooner, *History of Westchester County*, 467.
19. *Weekly Anglo-African*, "Revolutionary Incidents," 1.
20. *Weekly Anglo-African*, quoting Caleb Roscoe of the *Westchester Herald*, 2.
21. Ibid.

Chapter 4

22. Spooner, *Upon American and Foreign Grape Vines*, 68.
23. Rattroy, *East Hampton History*, 48.
24. Pickman, "Cultural Resources Survey, Croton Point Park," 60.
25. Spooner, *Upon American and Foreign Grape Vines*, 59.
26. Ibid., 47.
27. *New York Times*, "Season of the Vintage."
28. Spooner, *Upon American and Foreign Grape Vines*, 61.
29. Underhill, "Underhill Mill on the Croton," 44.
30. *New York Times*, "Underhill's Wines," 1.
31. Underhill, "Underhill Mill on the Croton," 44.
32. Ibid.
33. The website https://brickcollecting.com/history.htm will tell you everything you ever needed to know about bricks.
34. Marc Cheshire, village historian, Croton-on-Hudson, e-mail with author, December 10, 2021.
35. Pickman, "Cultural Resources Survey, Croton Point Park," 69.
36. *Geologist*, Tenth Annual Report of the State Geologist for the Year 1890, 124.
37. Ibid., 146.
38. *New York Times*, "Pierre Van Cortlandt Sells Croton Point Sand."

Chapter 5

39. May 1919 newspaper ad, from archives of Carl Oeschner.
40. *Rockland County Times*, "For Aero Protection of the Hudson Valley."
41. *New York Times*, "Suburban Transactions."
42. *Scarsdale Inquirer*, "CP May Be Purchased for Private Park."
43. *Croton Harmon News*, "Will Colored People Have Croton Point?"
44. *New York Times*, "Croton Point Sold to County for Park."
45. *White Plains Reporter*, "Croton Point Purchased by Westchester Park Committee."
46. *White Plains Reporter*, "Croton Beach Attracting Big Crowds."
47. *Scarsdale Inquirer*, "Two Hundred Children Gain Ton in Weight at Croton Camp."

48. Pickman, "Cultural Resources Survey, Croton Point Park," 77.
49. *New York Times*, "CROTON POINT SOLD TO COUNTY FOR PARK."

Chapter 6

50. Conversation with Clearwater crewmember, Ossining Waterfront.
51. DeChillo, "Environmentalists Press U.S."
52. Revkin, "Hill of Flowers Sprout Above Landfill."
53. Weaner, *Grassland Design & Management Specifications*.

Chapter 7

54. As documented and constantly updated by Hudson River Neptune himself, Tom Lake, DEC naturalist.
55. Henshaw, *Environmental History of the Hudson River*, 32.
56. New York State Department of Health, Hudson River & Tributaries Region fish advisories, health.ny.gov.
57. *New York Evening Post*, September 24, 1851.
58. *Scarsdale Inquirer*, "Pheasants Answer to Her Police Whistle."

BIBLIOGRAPHY

Aerial Age 15. "Uppercu, President of A.C.C. One of America's Most Enthusiastic Supporters of Aviation" (November 1922). https://archive.org/details/aerodigest1519unse_0/page/544/mode/2up.

Allen, J. Fisk. *A Practical Treatise of the Culture and Treatment of the Grape Vine.* 3rd ed. New York: C.M. Saxton, 1861.

Atkinson, J. Brooks. *East of the Hudson.* New York: Alfred A. Knopf, 1931.

Barnum, H.L. *The Spy Unmasked; Or, Memoirs of Enoch Crosby, Alia Harvey Birch, the Hero of Mr. Cooper's Tale of the Neutral Ground; Being an Authentic Account of the Secret Services Which He Rendered His Country during the Revolutionary War. Comprising Many Interesting Facts and Anecdotes, Never Before Published.* New York: J&J Harper, 1828.

Benson, Egbert. *Memoir, Read before the Historical Society of the State of New York, December 31, 1816.* New York, 1848.

Bierhorst, John, ed. *The White Deer and Other Stories Told by the Lenape.* N.p., 1995.

Binneweiss, Robert O. *Palisades: 1,000,000 Acres in 100 Years.* New York: Fordham University Press, 2001.

Bolton, Robert. *History of the County of Westchester.* New York: A.S. Gould, 1848.

Bolton, Robert, Jr. *A History of the County of Westchester from Its First Settlement to the Present Time.* Vol. 1. N.p., January 1, 1848.

Borkow, Richard. *George Washington's Westchester Gamble: The Encampment on the Hudson and the Trapping of Cornwallis.* Charleston, SC: The History Press, 2011.

Boyle, Robert. "From Mountaintop to 1,000 Fathoms Deep." *Sports Illustrated,* August 17, 1964.

Boyle, Robert H. *The Hudson River: A Natural and Unnatural History.* New York: Norton and Company, 1969.

Brennan, L.A. "The Lower Hudson: A Decade of Shell Middens." *Archaeology of Eastern North America,* no. 1 (1974): 81–93. http://www.jstor.org/stable/40897731.

Brennan, Louis A. *American Dawn : A New Model of American Prehistory.* New York: Macmillan Company, 1970.

————. *No Stone Unturned: An Almanac of North American Prehistory*. New York: Random House, 1959.

Brennan, Louis A., and Ingrid Fetz. *The Buried Treasure of Archaeology*. New York: Random House, 1964.

Brodhead, John Romeyn. *History of the State of New York: First Period, 1609–1664*. N.p., 1853.

Buckley, Edward H. "A Case for the Restoration of the Estuarine Ecosystem of Croton Bay/Croton River and Associated Tidal Marshes." *Estuarine Research in the 1980s*. Edited by C. Lavett Smith. Albany: State University of New York Press, 1992.

Bull, John. *Birds of the New York Area*. New York: Harper and Row, 1964.

Carey, Richard Adams. *The Philosopher Fish, Sturgeon, Caviar, and the Geography of Desire*. New York: Persues, 2005.

Case, Leslie. "The Lame Indian Chief." *Quarterly Bulletin of the Westchester Historical Society* 11, no. 3 (July 1935).

Chapdelaine, Claude, ed. *Late Pleistocene Archaeology & Ecology in the Far Northeast*. N.p.: Association des archéologues du Québec, 2012.

Chappelle, Howard I. *American Small Sailing Craft*. New York: Norton and Company, 1951.

Chazin, Daniel, ed. *New York Walk Book: A Companion to the New Jersey Walk Book*. 7th ed. Mahwah, NJ: New York-New Jersey Trail Conference, 2005.

Connolly, Colleen. "The True Native New Yorkers Can Never Truly Reclaim Their Homeland." *Smithsonian Magazine* (October 5, 2018).

Craven, Scott. "The Mouth of the Croton River: Dynamic Landscape in the Lower Hudson River Valley." Master's thesis, Western Connecticut State University, March 2007.

Cronin, John, and Kennedy, Robert F., Jr. *The Riverkeepers*. New York: Scribner's, 1997.

Croton Harmon News. "Will Colored People Have Croton Point?" August 10, 1923.

Croton, William. *Changes in the Land: Indians, Colonists and the Ecology of New England*. New York: Hill and Wang, 1983.

Danckaerts, Jasper, Peter Sluyter, Burleigh James Bartlett and J. Franklin Jameson. *Journal of Jasper Danckaerts, 1679–1680*. Bowie, MD: Heritage Books, 2001.

Daniels, Jane. *New York Walk Book*. 6th ed. New York: New York-New Jersey Trail Conference, 1998.

Daughan, George C. *Revolution on the Hudson: New York City and the Hudson River Valley in the American War of Independence*. New York: W.W. Norton & Company, 2016.

DeChillo, Suzanne. "Environmentalists Press U.S. on Issue of Croton Landfill." *New York Times*, January 26, 1986. https://nyti.ms/3BWxUgP.

————. "Fishermen's Group Keeps Pressure on County Over Dump," *New York Times*, August 3, 1986. https://nyti.ms/3C1ZrNY.

De Laet, Johannes. *Extracts of the New World, or A Description of the West Indies*. Cornell University Library Digital Collections, January 1, 1841. https://hdl.handle.net/2027/coo.31924067104855.

Department of Environmental Conservation. *Harmon Railroad Yard Wastewater Treatment Area, Westchester County, New York. Site number 3-60-010, RECORD OF DECISION. New York State Superfund, September 1992.*

Department of Environmental Conservation, Division of Hazardous Waste Remediation. *Croton Point Landfill, Site Number 36001, RECORD OF DECISION. Westchester County, New York. March 1993.*

Diamant, Lincoln. *Chaining the Hudson: The Fight for the River in the American Revolution.* New York: Fordham University Press, 2004.

Dublin, Susan, Dr. "Friends of Croton History Lecture Series." Croton Public Library, November 17, 2005.

Dunkak, Harry. "Winemaking in Westchester County: The Underhill Family of Croton." *Westchester Historian* 75, no. 3 (Summer 1999).

Dunne, Pete. *Pete Dunne on Bird Watching: The How-to, Where-to, and When-to of Birding.* New York: Houghton Mifflin, 2003.

Evjen, John O. *Scandinavian Immigrants in New York, 1630–1674; with Appendices on Scandinavians in Mexico and South America, 1532–1640, Scandinavians in Canada, 1619–1620, Some Scandinavians in New York in the Eighteenth Century, German Immigrants in New York, 1630–1674.* Minneapolis, MN: K.C. Holter, 1916. https://lccn.loc.gov/16006157.

Fabend, Firth Haring. *New Netherland in a Nutshell.* N.p.: New Netherland Institute, 2012.

Fava, J.F. "Croton Point Park Compilation of History & Points of Interest for Interpretative Signing." Report for Westchester County Department of Parks, Recreation & Conservation, 2003.

Ferris, Marc. "The Truck Stops Here." *New York Times*, November 10, 2002. https://nyti.ms/3M5H5A1.

Fiedel, Stuart. "Archaic and Woodland Occupations at Teller's Point." *The Archeology and Ethnohistory of the Lower Hudson Valley and Neighboring Regions: Essays in Honor of Louis A. Brennan.* No. 11. Edited by Herbert Kraft. N.p.: Occasional Publications in Northeastern Anthropology, 1991.

Flores, Dan. *Coyote America: A Natural & Supernatural History.* New York: Basic Books, 2016.

Funk, Robert E. *Recent Contributions to Hudson Valley Prehistory.* Albany: University of the State of New York, State Education Department, 1976.

Galusha, Diane. *Liquid Assets: A History of New York's Water System.* Fleischmanns, NY: Purple Mountain Press, 1999.

Geologist. Tenth Annual Report of the State Geologist for the Year 1890 (Classic Reprint). New York: FB&C Limited, 2017.

Giddy, Ian H., and Scott Keller. *The Official Guide to the Hudson River Greenway Water Trail.* New York: Hudson River Water Trail Association Inc., 2015.

Gordon, John Steele. "Inventing the Bird Business." *New York Times*, December, 1996.

Grave, Marian. "Wampum Strings of the Kitchawancs" Unpublished manuscript, Croton Historical Society, 1952.

Greene, Donna. "County Seeks Way to Harvest Methane Gas at Landfill." *New York Times*, December 6, 1998. https://nyti.ms/3vvPTcu.

Griffin, Ernest Freeland, ed. *Westchester and Its People*. Vol. 2. N.p., 1946.

Griffin, Phillip R. "Whaleboats on the Hudson." *Journal of the American Revolution* (October 12, 2017).

Grumet, Robert S. *First Manhattans: A Brief History of the Munsee*. Norman: University of Oklahoma Press, 2011.

———. *Historic Contact: Indian People and Colonists in Today's Northeastern US in the 16th–18th Centuries*. Norman: University of Oklahoma Press, 1995.

———. *The Munsee Indians: A History*. Norman: University of Oklahoma Press, 2009.

Hadamy, William, ed. *The McDonald Papers Parts 1 & 2*. White Plains, NY: Westchester Historical Society, 1926.

Hall, John. *Tenth Annual Report of the State Geologist for the Year 1890*. N.p.: Forgotten Books, 2017.

Harrington, Mark. Report Concerning Archeological Investigations at Croton-on-Hudson, Westchester County, New York. August 15–September 20, 1899.

Heckenwelder, Reverend John. *A Narrative of the Mission of the United Brethren Among the Delaware and Mohegan Indians*. Philadelphia, PA: McCarty & Davis, 1820.

Hedrick, U.P., and Nathaniel Ogden Booth. *The Grapes of New York*. Albany, NY: J.B. Lyon Company, 1908. https://archive.org/details/grapesofnewyork00hedr.

Henshaw, Robert E., ed. *Environmental History of the Hudson River: Human Uses that Changed the Ecology, Ecology that Changed Human Uses*. New York: State University of New York Press, 2011.

Heron, Jim. *Denning's Point: A Hudson History*. Hensonville, NY: Black Dome Press, 2006.

Higgins, Alvin. "The Story of Croton." *Quarterly Bulletin of the Westchester County Historical Society* 16, no. 3 (July 1940).

Hoffman, Renoda. "The Night the Dam Broke." *Westchester Historian, Quarterly of the Westchester County Historical Society* 44, no. 4 (Fall 1968).

Hollway, Marjorie. "Hudson River Commercial Fisherman's Oral History Collection." Hudson River Maritime Museum, conducted between 1989 and 2000. Digital archives.

Horecky, Scott. "Ft. Kitchawanc Archeological Preserve at Croton Point." Mohican Seminar 3, The Journey—An Algonquian Peoples Seminar. Edited by Shirley Dunn. Bulletin, No. 511. University of the State of New York, Albany, New York, 2009.

Hudson River and the Hudson River Rail-Road with Complete Map and Wood Cut Views of the Principal Objects of Interest Upon the Line. New York: W.C. Lodre & Company, 1851.

Humes, Edward. *Garbology: Our Dirty Love Affair with Trash*. New York: Avery, 2013.

Hutton, George V. *The Great Hudson River Brick Industry: Commemorating Three and a Half Centuries of Brickmaking*. Fleischmans, NY: Purple Mountain Press, 2003.

Irvington Gazette. "Point Pleasant Park." June 14, 1912.

Jacobs, Jaap. *New Netherland: A Dutch Colony in 17th Century America*. N.p.: Brill, 2004.

Jameson, J. Franklin, ed. *Narratives of New Netherland, 1609–1664*. New York: Charles Scribner and Sons, 1909. https://babel.hathitrust.org/cgi/pt?id=loc.ark:/13960/t9c53v237&view=1up&seq=9&skin=20.

Johnson, James M., Christopher Pryslopski and Andréw Vallni, eds. *Key to the Northern Country: The Hudson River Valley in the American Revolution.* New York: State University of New York Press, 2013.

Juet, Robert. *Juet's Journal of Hudson's 1609 Voyage, from the 1625 Edition of Purchas His Pilgrimes.* New Jersey Historical Society, 1959.

Kendall, David L. *Glaciers and Granite: A Guide to Maine's Landscape & Geology.* Unity, ME: North County Press, 1993.

Ketchum, Richard M. *Saratoga: Turning Point of America's Revolutionary War.* New York: Henry Holt, 1997.

Kilgannon, Corey. "Was that a Manatee in the Hudson, or Just a Fat Log?" *New York Times*, August 8, 2006.

Kiviat, E. *Phragmites Management Sourcebook for the Tidal Hudson River: Report to the Hudson River Foundation.* Annandale, NY: Hudsonia Ltd., 2006

Koeppel, Gerard T. *Water for Gotham: A History.* Princeton, NJ: Princeton University Press, 2000.

Koke, Richard J. *Accomplice in Treason: Joshua Hett Smith and the Arnold Conspiracy.* New York: New York Historical Society, 1973.

Kraft, Herbert, ed. "The Archeology and Ethnohistory of the Lower Hudson Valley and Neighboring Regions: Essays in Honor of Louis A. Brennan." *Occasional Publications in Northeastern Anthropology*, no. 11 (1991).

Kurlansky, Mark. *The Big Oyster: History on the Half Shell.* New York: Ballantine Books, 2006.

Lederer, Richard M. *The Place Names of Westchester County.* Harrison, NY: Harbor Hill Books, 1972.

Lenik, Edward J. *Lost Arrowheads and Broken Pottery: A History of Native Americans in Bear Mountain State Park, New York.* New York: Purple Mountain Press, 2010.

Letts, Chris. "Shad and the Men Who Fished for Them." *Westchester Historian* 66, no. 1 (Winter 1990).

Lewis, Tom. *The Hudson: A History.* New Haven: Yale University Press, 2005.

Lifset, Robert D. *Power on the Hudson, Storm King Mountain and the Emergence of Modern American Environmentalism.* Pittsburgh, PA: University of Pittsburgh Press, 2014.

Lipman, Andrew. *The Saltwater Frontier, Indians and the Contest for the American Coast.* New Haven, CT: Yale University Press, 2015.

Lossing, Benson. *The Hudson: The Wilderness to the Sea.* N.p.: Franklin Classics, 2018. Originally published in 1866.

Lothrop, Jonathan C., Darrin L. Lowery, Arthur E. Spiess and Christopher J. Ellis. "Early Human Settlement of Northeastern North America." *PaleoAmerica* 2, no. 3 (2016): 192–251.

Macfarlane, Robert. *Landmarks.* United Kingdom: Penguin Random House, 2015.

Markl, Rudi G. "Pleistocene Geology of Croton Point, New York." Reprinted from *Transactions of the New York Academy of Sciences.* Series 2, vol. 33, no. 55.

Martin, Joseph Plumb. *A Narrative of Some of the Adventures, Dangers and Sufferings of a Revolutionary Soldier Interspersed with Anecdotes of Incidents that Occurred within His Own Observation.* N.p.: Glaziers, Masters & Company, 1830.

McHugh, Christopher Michael. "UN Headquarters in Croton." *Ossining-Croton-On-Hudson Patch,* July 13, 2012.

McPhee, John. *The Founding Fish.* New York: Farrar, Straus and Giroux, 2002.

Melvin, Tessa. "County Plans a 'Fast Track' Cap for the Landfill." *New York Times,* December 2, 1990.

Mergurian, Charles, and John E. Sanders. *Trips on the Rocks, Guide 09: Geology of Croton Point and Peekskill Hollow, NY.* Trip 10: May 12, 1990; Trip 25: November 1992.

Minetor, Randi. *Falcon Guides/Hiking New York's Lower Hudson Valley.* New York: Globe Pequot, 2018.

Moulton, Joseph W., and John V.N. Yates. *History of the State of NY: Including the Aboriginal and Colonial Annals.* New York: A.T. Goodrich, 1824. https://archive.org/details/historyofstateof12moul_0.

New York Times. "Airport for Westchester: Supervisors Vote $53,000 to Buy Land Near Croton Point Park." August 6, 1929.

———. "Croton Point May Be Site of New Park." June 19, 1923.

———. "CROTON POINT SOLD TO COUNTY FOR PARK; Westchester Acquires 300-Acre Tract for Price Said to Be $360,000. NEGRO BIDDERS LOSE OUT Harlem Group Negotiated for Land to Build Resort for Their Race." August 28, 1923. https://nyti.ms/3tbnNkk.

———. "An Explosion Kills Four." October 21, 1899. https://nyti.ms/35fGX0j.

———. "Fear Ship Rowdies Caused Drowning, Police Told that Excursionists Leaped into the River After Ruffians Caused Craft to Ground." September 18, 1926. https://nyti.ms/3Maq080.

———. "A Kidnap Suspect Leads a 21-Car Chase." April 11, 1988. https://nyti.ms/3M61BRc.

———. "Pierre Van Cortlandt Sells Croton Point Sand." September 26, 1874. https://nyti.ms/3tbrwyk.

———. "The Season of the Vintage." October 23, 1862. https://nyti.ms/3htxxkp.

———. "Suburban Transactions: Corporation Buys 350-Acre Tract at Croton for Airplane Landing." December 15, 1921.

———. "Underhill's Wines." December 25, 1864. https://nyti.ms/3HyJhgc.

Northshield, Jane, ed. *History of Croton-on-Hudson, New York.* The Croton-on-Hudson Bicentennial Celebration Committee, 1976.

O'Brien, Raymond J. *American Sublime: Landscape and Scenery of the Lower Hudson Valley.* New York: Columbia University Press, 1981.

O'Callaghan, Edmund. *History of New Netherland: Or, NY Under the Dutch.* New York: D. Appleton & Company, 1848. https://archive.org/details/historyofnewneth01ocal/page/n13/mode/2up?ref=ol&view=theater.

Owen, James. "The Fortified Indian Village at CP." *Quarterly Bulletin of the Westchester County Historical Society* 2, no. 2 (April 1926).

———. "Indian Occupation of Croton Neck and Point." *Quarterly Bulletin of the Westchester County Historical Society* 1, no. 4 (October 1925).

Panetta, Roger, ed. *Dutch New York: The Roots of Hudson Valley Culture.* New York: Fordham University Press, 2009.

Parker, Arthur C. "The Archeological History of New York." *New York State Museum Bulletin*, nos. 237, 238 (September–October 1920).

Patterson, Emma L. *Peekskill in the American Revolution*. Peekskill, NY: Friendly Town Association Inc., 1944.

Peteet, Dorothy M., et al. "Hudson River Paleoecology from Marshes: Environmental Change and Its Implications for Fisheries." American Fisheries Symposium 51. American Fisheries Society, 2006, 113–28.

Peterson, Roger Tory. *Peterson Field Guide to Birds of Eastern and Central North America*. New York: Houghton & Mifflin, 2020.

Philbrick, Nathaniel. *Valiant Ambition: George Washington, Benedict Arnold, and the Fate of the American Revolution*. New York: Viking, 2016.

Pickman, Arnold. "Cultural Resources Survey, Croton Point Park, Westchester County, New York." Draft Report, Cragsmoor Consultants, 2004.

Pierson, Frank H. "The Crawbucky Tales." Westchester Archives, n.d. https://westchesterarchives.com/ht/muni/wchs/crawbucky.html.

Public Archaeology Laboratory. "New Discoveries at Old Place: The Story of the Old Place Neck Site, Staten Island, New York." 2012. https://www.palinc.com/sites/default/files/publications/Old_Place_Neck_Site.pdf.

Purple, Edwin R. *Contributions to the History of Ancient Families of New Amsterdam & New York*. New York: privately printed, 1881.

Rattroy, Jeannette Edwards. *East Hampton History*. Garden City, NY: Country Life Press, 1953.

Revkin, Andrew C. "Hill of Flowers Sprout Above Landfill." *New York Times*, June 2, 1995. https://nyti.ms/3BYkErN.

Reynolds, Richard J. *Hydrogeology of the Croton-Ossining Area, Westchester County, New York*. Water-Resources Investigations Report 87-4159. U.S. Geological Survey, 1988. https://doi.org/10.3133/wri874159.

Ritchie, William A. *Archeology of New York State*. New York: Harbor Hill Books, 1965.

Rockland County Times. "For Aero Protection of the Hudson Valley." January 26, 1918.

Rondthaler, Edward. "Friends of Croton History Lecture Series." Croton Public Library, June 2, 2005.

———. "Friends of Croton History Lecture Series." Croton Public Library, June 17, 1997.

Rosenthal, Elizabeth J. *Bird-Watcher: The Life of Roger Tory Peterson*. Guilford, CT: Rowman & Littlefield, 2008.

Route, Elizabeth. *Garbage Land: On the Secret Trail of Trash*. New York: Back Bay Books, 2005.

Ruttenber, E.M. *History of the Indian Tribes of Hudson's River: Their Origin, Manner and Customs; Tribal and Sub-Tribal Organizations; Wars, Treaties, etc., etc.* Albany, NY: J. Munsell, 1872. https://archive.org/details/ruttenberindians00ruttrich/page/n11/mode/2up.

Sanders, J.E., and Charles Merguerian. "The Glacial Geology of New York City and Vicinity." *The Geology of Staten Island, New York, Field Guide and Proceedings*. Edited by A.I. Benimoff. The Geological Association of New Jersey, XI Annual Meeting, 1994.

Sanderson, Eric W. *Mannahatta: A Natural History of New York City*. New York: Abrams, 2009.

Scarsdale Inquirer. "Croton Point May Be Purchased for Private Park." August 18, 1923.

———. "Pheasants Answer to Her Police Whistle." September 10, 1926.

———. "Revives Tradition of Captain Kidd's Famous Buried Treasure." December 13, 1924.

———. "Two Hundred Children Gain Ton in Weight at Croton Camp." December 5, 1925.

Scharf, J. Thomas. *History of Westchester County*. Philadelphia, PA: L.E. Preston & Company, 1886.

Schecter, Barnett. *The Battle for New York: The City at the Heart of the American Revolution*. New York: Walker & Company, 2002.

Schimmrich, Steven. *Geology of the Hudson Valley: A Billion Years of History*. N.p.: independently published, 2020.

Schonnard, Frederic, and W.W. Spooner. *History of Westchester County*. New York: New York History Company, 1900. https://archive.org/details/historyofwestche00inshon/page/n7/mode/2up.

Schoolcraft, H. Rowe., and F.S. (Francis Samuel) Drake. *The Indian Tribes of the United States: Their History Antiquities, Customs, Religion, Arts, Language, Traditions, Oral Legends, and Myths*. Philadelphia, PA: Lippincott, 1884.

Sheehan, Michael J. "An American Perspective on the Guard Boats of the Hudson." *Journal of the American Revolution* (October 23, 2017).

Sheng, Peter Y., et al. "Invasive Phragmites Provides Superior Wave and Surge Damage Protection Relative to Native Plants during Storms." *Environment. Res. Lett.* 16 054008 (2021).

Shorto, Russell. *Island at the Center of the World*. New York: Abacus, 2001.

Sirkin, Les, D.H. Cadwell and G.G. Connally. "Pleistocene Geology of the Eastern, Lower Hudson River Valley, New York." Report. New York State Geology Association, 1989. https://www.nysga-online.org/wp-content/uploads/2019/06/NYSGA-1989-B5-Pleistocene-Geology-of-the-Eastern-Lower-Hudson-Valley-New-York.pdf.

Smith, C. Lavett. *Fish Watching: An Outdoor Guide to Freshwater Fishes*. Ithaca, NY: Cornell University Press, 1994.

Smith, Joshua Hett. *An Authentic Narrative of the Causes Which Led to the Death of Major André, Adjutant-General of His Majesty's Forces in North America*. London: Matthews and Leigh, 1808.

———. *Record of the Trial of Joshua Hett Smith, Esq.: For Alleged Complicity in the Treason of Benedict Arnold: 1780*. Morrisania, NY: Readstreet Press, 1866.

Spooner, Alden. *Upon American and Foreign Grapevines*. 2nd ed. Brooklyn, NY, 1858.

Staudter, Thomas. "The Birdman of Ossining." *Hudson Valley Magazine* (August 4, 2008).

Stilgoe, John R. *Outside Lies Magic: Regaining History and Awareness in Everyday Places*. New York: Walker & Company, 1998.

Stockbridge-Munsee Band of Mohican Indians. "Resource Guide." https://www.mohican.com/services/cultural-services/cultural-affairs/faq.

Striebach, Jim. "How Peekskill Solved Westchester's Waste Problem: A Ten-Year Tale of Trash, Sludge, Power and Politics." *Peekskill Herald*, April 8, 2021.

Tekiela, Stan. *Majestic Eagles: Compelling Facts and Images of the Bald Eagle*. Cambridge, MN: Adventure Publications, 2007.

Tessa, Melvin. "County Plans a 'Fast Track' Cap for the Landfill." *New York Times*, December 2, 1990.

Thorson, Robert M. *Beyond Walden: The Hidden History of America's Kettle Lakes and Ponds*. New York: Walker Publishing, 2009.

Titus, Robert, and Joanna Titus. *The Hudson Valley in the Ice Age: A Geological History and Tour*. New York: Black Dome Press Corporation, 2012.

Town of Cortlandt Bicentennial History Committee. *History of the Town of Cortlandt*. Croton-on-Hudson, NY: Graphic Harmony, 1988.

Underhill, Frederick. "The Underhill Mill on the Croton." *Quarterly Bulletin of the Westchester County Historical Society* 23, nos. 3–4 (July–October 1947).

Underhill, Sarah. "A Brief History of Croton Point." Westchester Historical Society, 2001.

Van der Donck, Adriaen, Charles T. Gehring and William A. Starna. *A Description of New Netherland*. Lincoln: University of Nebraska Press, 2010.

Van Diver, Bradford B. *Roadside Geology of New York*. Missoula, MT: Mountain Press, 1985.

Van Laer, Arnold J., ed. and trans. Documents Relating to New Netherland, 1624–1626. Henry E. Huntingdon Library and Art Gallery, 1924.

Van Laer, Arnold J.F. *New York Historical Manuscripts: Dutch*. Baltimore, MD: Genealogical Publishing Company, 1974.

Waldman, John. *Running Silver, Restoring Atlantic Rivers and Their Great Fish Migrations*. Guilford, CT: Lyons Press, 2013.

Weaner, Larry. *Grassland Design & Management Specifications, Croton Point Park Croton-on-Hudson, NY.* Westchester County Department of Parks, Recreation & Conservation, October 19, 2015.

Weekly Anglo-African. "Revolutionary Incidents." October 15, 1859.

Weidensaul, Scott. *Of a Feather: A Brief History of American Birding*. New York: Harcourt, 2007.

Weiselberg, Erik, PhD. "Revolutionary Westchester: John 'Jack' Peterson." *Hudson River Independent*, August 27, 2020.

———. "Revolutionary Westchester: John Odell, General Washington's Westchester Guide." *Revolutionary Westchester* 250 (2020).

Weslager, C.A. *The Delaware Indians: A History*. New Brunswick, NJ: Rutgers University Press, 1991.

White Plains Reporter. "Croton Beach Attracting Big Crowds." July 19, 1922.

———. "Croton Point Purchased by Westchester Park Committee." August 28, 1923.

Wilkinson, Alec. *The Riverkeeper*. New York: Knopf, 1991.

Wyckof, Jerome. *Rock Scenery of the Hudson Highlands and Palisades*. Glenn's Falls, NY: Appalachian Mountain Club, 1971.

INDEX

ABOUT THE AUTHORS

SCOTT CRAVEN is a former Ossining police captain whose master's thesis focused on an environmental history of the area. As the historian of the Town of Ossining and an avid fisherman, paddler and cyclist, he knows the point better than most. Over the years, he has naturally connected with many people whose passion and expertise regarding different aspects of the point have helped us weave its history into a compelling story.

CAROLINE RANALD CURVAN is professional researcher and writer. She recently led the research team for the critically acclaimed American Masters/PBS documentary *Laura Ingalls Wilder: Prairie to Page*. A writer with popular local blog (OssiningHistoryontheRun.com) and an adjunct professor of research and composition, she is a deep and passionate student of history.

Visit us at
www.historypress.com